CEREDIGION

Ceredigion Walks

Richard Sale

ISBN: 0-86381-603-7

Cover photo: Aberaeron (Bwrdd Croeso Cymru)

Cover design: Alan Jones

First published in 2000 by
Gwasg Carreg Gwalch, 12 Iard yr Orsaf, Llanrwst, Wales LL26 0EH
℡ 01492 642031 📠 01492 641502
📧 books@carreg-gwalch.co.uk   website: www.carreg-gwalch.co.uk

Contents

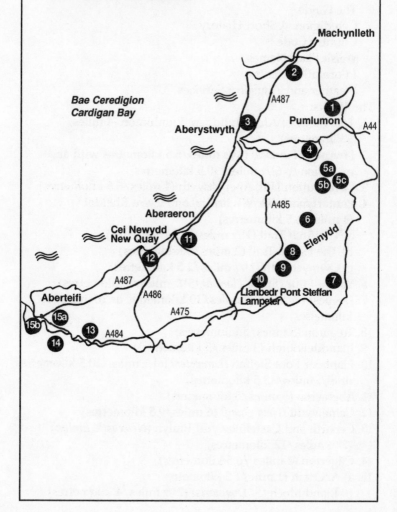

Location Map
of the Walks

Machynlleth

Bae Ceredigion
Cardigan Bay

Aberystwyth

Pumlumon

A487

A44

A485

Aberaeron

Cei Newydd
New Quay

Elenydd

A487

A486

Aberteifi

A475

Llanbedr Pont Steffan
Lampeter

A484

① ② ③ ④ ⑤a ⑤b ⑤c ⑥ ⑦ ⑧ ⑨ ⑩ ⑪ ⑫ ⑬ ⑭ ⑮a ⑮b

Introduction

The Guide

One of the aims of this guide is simplicity. Walks are easy to follow, and clear directions are given. Another aim is variety. Walks have been selected that will highlight Ceredigion's outstanding history and scenic beauty. The exact location for the starting point of each walk is given, and how to get there.

Walks vary in length from 1.5 miles/2.5 kilometres to 10 miles/16 kilometres. In general the walks are well maintained and clearly signposted. Those who are uncertain of how long a walk of given length will take should use the Naismith Formula, a well-known walking aid. This suggests a time of one hour for every 3 map miles (or five map kilometres) covered, plus an additional half-hour for each 1,000 feet (300m) of ascent. The map distance is quoted for each of the walks: none of the walks in the guide involve significant climbing.

Sketch maps for each walk are provided; however they can not substitute for the definitive OS (Ordnance Survey) maps. The relevant Landranger (1:50,000) sheets and Explorer or Outdoor Leisure (1;25,000) sheets are given for each walk.

The grading system used is largely self-explanatory. Easy walks involve short walks over easy terrain, with limited climbing. Moderate walks are either longer, may have more climbing, or more complicated route finding. The Difficult routes are much longer or involve other, significant, difficulties.

For each walk, 'refreshments' indicate whether food and drink are available on, or close to, the route. Those villages or towns noted as offering a good range of refreshments are also likely to have public toilets and to offer accommodation. For a full list of accommodation options, contact the local Tourist Information Office.

Public transport (or its absence) to the start points is noted, though bus times should always be checked before starting out as services may be restricted to a few (or even just one) bus per day.

7

Apart from Walks 1 and 7 none of the routes cross an upland area exposed to the weather. The remaining walks are low level and rarely remote. Nevertheless, all the walks will seem long and arduous to those ill-equipped for rain, cold or wind. Please ensure you are wearing or carrying adequate clothing and have proper footwear. And please remember to follow the Country Code.

Ceredigion: A Short History

In a book of history walks, it seems inappropriate to also have a chapter dedicated to the history of Ceredigion. But Ceredigion is so important to the history of Wales that an overview of Welsh history is needed to place the historical snap-shots given in the walks in context. Ceredigion was – and to an extent still is – the borderland between the Welsh heartland of Gwynedd, the stronghold of the Welsh language, and the more 'English' land of southern Pembroke, a position which caused consternation when the new county of Dyfed was formed. During the author's time at University College of Wales, Aberystwyth the debate over language seemed to wash over the town as frequently as the tide across the beach. Today, with a parliament established and national identity more secure, Ceredigion has re-emerged as being distinctly Welsh. It is a fine county with a wonderful array of landscapes. It does not have the high jagged peaks of Snowdonia, but Pumlumon and Elenydd, the high plateau of mid-Wales, offer the same solitude and wildness. It has a superb coastline, lovely river valleys, lush pastoral scenery and a collection of inspiring towns and valleys. It is a joy for the walker.

Ceredigion may have been occupied by man for 250,000 years, though that occupation, here as elsewhere, has not been continuous; the ice ages pushing polar ice southwards and forcing man to retreat over the land bridge that joined what is now south-eastern England to the continent. The earliest occupation has not resulted in recognisable remains: earliest man left few clues to his existence, and what he left may well have been rubbed away by the glaciers. The first remains so far discovered of man in Wales are from the Palaeolithic (Old Stone) Age, remains which are perhps 20,000 years old. The best of these are of the so-called Red Lady of Paviland, the skeletal remains (actually of a man, the bones stained with red ochre) found on the Gower. As Palaeolithic man was a hunter, it is probable that hunters who were in the Gower (and those who occupied a cave near Tenby where other remains have been found) would have made their way north to Ceredigion's valleys and coast.

Palaeolithic remains are rare, in part because of the minimal use of tools which survive periods of 20,000 years or so, in part because although the folk were cave dwellers, they may not have always left the bodies of the dead close to the living. It is also likely that the settlement of the county was minimal: the ice ages were still grumbling on, with much of northern Britain being Arctic tundra and even the south a cold place, a difficult place to survive. It is possible that only the coastal plain of Wales was habitable and, as there are few suitable living places in that area of the county, it is unlikely that Ceredigion's resident population was large.

But the climate was improving. The ice moved north and, behind it, forests started to colonise the tundra. More animals crossed the land bridge from Europe and with them came more advanced folk, a people who could start to leave their mark on the landscape. Neolithic (New Stone Age) folk buried their dead – the important ones at least – in chambers built of stone slabs, which they earthed over to form long barrows. Time sometimes blew the earth away, leaving behind a dolmen (or cromlech as it is known in Welsh). There are no good examples in Ceredigion, but there is a collection of very fine tombs just to the south of Aberteifi.

The Bronze Age brought a change of burial ritual, with the

9

introduction of cremation and the internment of ashes in cairns or round barrows. The Bronze Age was also the age of standing stones – though this might have been a continuation of earlier practice. The Welsh for a standing stone is *maen hir* (long stone), and it is that name, shortened to menhir, that has become popular in describing such stones. Lately, with the increased coverage – not all of it useful – given to astro-archaeology, menhirs have taken on a considerable significance. It is now possible to view the stones as markers of extraterrestrial air terminals, batteries holding mystical power, or connections for large energy reservoirs. While such 'earth magic' ideas may be too fanciful, it is easy to understand the emotional tug of such stones. There are excellent examples of round barrows in Ceredigion – near Cilcennin, Tregaron and Ponterwyd, and Bedd Taliesin near Talybont, so named because it was long believed to be the grave of the legendary 6th century poet – but no significant standing stone sites (the stone circle at Ysbyty Cynfyn to the north of Pontarfynach (Devil's Bridge) has had stones removed to act as gateposts and building material for the nearby church, and is now too removed from its original form to be of great value to archaeologists), though again there are good examples over the county boundary to the south of Aberteifi.

The replacement of the Bronze Age culture in Wales by the Iron Age people appears to have been by intermixing rather than annihilation. This theory rests on two bases: first the finding, in Llyn Fawr, Morgannwg (Glamorgan), of a hoard of metal objects, some of bronze, some of iron and yet of, apparently, contemporary manufacture and usage; and secondly, and more romantically, the possibility of a real folk memory behind the story of the lady of the lake at Llyn y Fan Fach near Y Mynydd Du, the most easterly mountain block of the Brecon Beacons National Park. The Iron Age in Wales was deeply significant as it represented the coming of the peoples whose name is synonymous with the country – the Celts.

To the civilised Romans and Greeks of Mediterranean Europe, the Celts were barbarians and war-like savages. Civilisation, of course, is comparative – it is true that the Celts did not possess written literature but their oral traditions has now been recognised as one of the richest in European history. The Roman expansion into northern Europe was probably motivated as much by frequent attacks from the Celts on their border as by any expansionist dreams. The Romans were impressed by the qualities of the Celts in battle, but unimpressed by what they saw as the puerile boasting of their leaders, parading about in ornaments accompanied by men forever chanting their praises. They did not at first realise the true significance of what they saw. The Celts, having no literature, had invested the history of their peoples in epic poems that were remembered and delivered by bards. This had two direct results. Firstly a heroic leader stock was created which continually broadcast their own, and their ancestors', heroism. Thus a leader who was not rich and majestic, and not celebrated in the bardic poems, was suspect and might not protect you well enough. Secondly, a love of language for its own sake developed. To such an extent was this true that the Celts actually had a god of eloquence – Ogmios. Eventually the Romans and Greeks recognised this eloquence for what it was. The Celts maintained, in essence, that the tongue was mightier than the sword and they venerated age which increased its powers. Eventually they emerged in the classical world as teachers of rhetoric.

The Celtic tribes had invaded Britain at an early time and were well established when the Romans came: there are several examples in Ceredigion of their typical hill fort, most famously at Pen Dinas close to Aberystwyth. In 43AD the Romans subdued the Celts of southern England after many bloody battles, but one tribal leader, Caratacus (Caradog), escaped to Wales where he rallied the Silures of south Wales and the Ordovices of the north. He fought on until AD51 when he was

11

betrayed and captured. It seems that his fighting ability and his bearing after capture so impressed the Romans that he died peacefully as an honoured guest of Rome. The Romans built large forts at Caerleon and Chester to police the Celts of Wales and marched on Ynys Môn (Anglesey) to negate the threat of the druids, but there are very limited remains from west Wales. There was a significant town (Moridunum) where Carmarthen now stands, forts near Llandovery and, of course, the gold mines of Dolaucothi near Pumpsaint. but these, and a scattering of others, are isolated instances.

After the Romans conquest Britain was quiet for several centuries, the local Brythonic tribes becoming Romanised and the basis of the present system of roads and towns being created. When the Romans finally withdrew, however, the Brythons proved that they had learnt little in the occupation years and there was an immediate return to tribalism with new kings emerging to do battle with each other. Such a system of small states with little cohesion and occasional open hostility was easy to deal with, and the Anglo-Saxon invaders (who were initially brought to Britain – so legend has it – as mercenaries to assist one Brython king against another) pushed the Brythons/Cymry farther and farther west after the Romans departed. The Saxon advance was halted for a while – possibly by the legendary King Arthur – but in 577 they won the battle of Dyrham, near Bristol, cutting the country in half and banishing the Brythons to Cornwall and Wales. The Saxons saw the British to the west of the Severn as the Wallas – foreigners, a name deriving from another Celtic tribe, the Velcae. The Brythons, now isolated from their own kind, increasingly stopped referring to themselves as Brythons (Britons), being instead 'fellow countrymen' – Cymry.

The *foreigners* of Wales were now left in peace while the Saxons moved northward to secure that border. This was a long process and the Saxons lost interest in westward expansion. Eventually an effective demarcation line was set up between

Saxon England and Wales by the construction of a boundary dyke by the Mercian king Offa, though the true reason for its construction is not known.

Behind the dyke the Welsh were embracing Christianity, a succession of Celtic saints evangelising the country following the time of the Roman departure. Some of the finest remains from this period of Welsh history – carved and inscribed gravestones – are to be found in west Wales, including, at Llanddewi Brefi (Walk 9) one of the earliest references to Dewi Sant (St David). This reference is apt as it was at this Ceredigion village that Dewi spoke at a synod which decided the direction of Welsh Christianity, a speech attended by miracles which proved both his own sainthood and the correctness of his vision of the future.

But despite the conversion to Christianity the Celts also continued to fight among themselves, no ruler of one of the great kingdoms – Gwynedd, Powys, Dyfed, Deheubarth, Gwent – being able to unify the country. The northern kingdoms were occasionally brought under one man's control, but the southern counties, and particularly Gwent, maintained a stubborn independence. Eventually Gruffudd, son of Llywelyn ap Seisyllt, did unify the country, in 1041, but he over-reached himself, seeking allegiances with Saxon lords near the dyke, probably in an effort to expand eastward. Earl Harold Godwinson convinced Edward the Confessor that the Welsh king represented a threat and received permission to move against him. Earl Harold invaded Wales driving Gruffudd into hiding. The abandoned Gruffudd was murdered in August 1063.

Following Gruffudd's defeat Wales fragmented again and by the time the Normans arrived at the dyke there was once more a system of small, usually squabbling kingdoms on its western side.

The Normans did not attempt a conquest of Wales (in the way they conquered England that is), it apparently not being part of William's plan for his new realm. Instead the Conqueror installed a line of barons on the march, or boundary, of England and Wales. These lords ruled virtually independent states, and their westward boundaries were of their own choosing. Consequently they encroached on Welsh land perpetually, gradually pushing the 'free' Welsh back. Had the marcher lords confined themselves to the eastern border between England and Wales (a border more or less defined by Offa's Dyke – and by the present border), history might have been different. But the Normans also thrust deep into south Wales which, by virtue of its lower, flatter country, was more accessible. The 'march', between Norman England was thus an arc rather than a line, from Chester to Chepstow and westwards towards Pembroke, but reaching north as far as Aberteifi.

An attempt by the Normans to push northwards, across Afon Teifi ended in defeat at the battle of Crug Mawr in 1136, a battle which helped define the Welsh kingdom of Deheubarth, which included Ceredigion. By the mid-12th century the kingdom was ruled by Rhys ap Gruffudd (or Yr Arglwydd Rhys), but he was required, reluctantly, to accept Henry II as his overlord. Then, in 1165 when Henry moved against Owain Gwynedd in north Wales, Rhys took advantage of the confusion to expand the borders of Deheubarth. He took Cilgerran (see Walk 14) and built castles at Rhayader and Cydweli, and even attacked the Norman castle at Swansea, but he was never able to subdue the pro-Norman communities of Pembroke. The early Norman kings had imported Flemish craftsmen to an ethically cleansed south-west Wales to establish wool and other cottage industries, and the allegiance of these communities was to their Norman protectors rather than the Welsh princes. The existence of this 'little England beyond Wales' was to prove disastrous to all future Welsh princes.

In the north, Owain Gwynedd pushed the Normans back in Powys, but was defeated and forced back. Owain's death, and that of Rhys in 1197, caused power struggles and a weakening of Gwynedd, the most powerful of the Welsh kingdoms, and Deheubarth. Owain's grandson, Llywelyn ap Iorwerth (Llywelyn Fawr) succeeded to the kingdom of Gwynedd in 1203 and strengthened it. He conquered Powys and by siding with the English barons gained rights for Wales in Magna Carta. He skilfully exploited the divisions among Rhys's descendants to gain control over Deheubarth and had successes in south Wales where he assisted the Marcher lord Richard Marshall to recover Usk castle from Henry III. When Llywelyn died in 1240 Wales, while not unified, had a truly independent air. The position of the south-west, and also of Gwent, was still ambiguous, but the co-operation, however suspicious, between the Marcher lords and the Welsh leaders making full support for an independent Wales grudging at best.

In the wake of Llywelyn's death Wales fragmented again. His grandson, Llywelyn ap Gruffudd (Llywelyn the Last), campaigned again for Welsh unity. He demanded, and received, the title of Prince of Wales from Henry III under the treaty of Montgomery of 1267, but the king's son, Edward I, was made of sterner stuff than his predecessors. He invaded Wales, forcing a submission and homage from Llywelyn and imposing, with the Treaty of Aberconwy in 1277, a reduction of Llywelyn's position to that of a baron. In 1282 Llywelyn rose again, but only briefly, being killed in a minor skirmish near Builth Wells.

Edward built the castles of the 'Ring of Stone' to enforce English dominance. He also systematically removed the lineage of the Welsh royal houses by forcing women into nunneries and preventing men from producing heirs by long-term imprisonment or death. Edward's imposed peace lasted 100 years before being shattered by the rising of Owain Glyndŵr. It is ironic that the Flemings of south-west Wales, whose placing was intended to make the unification of Wales so difficult for the Welsh princes, were now to precipitate Glyndŵr's rising (see Walk 1).

The failure of Glyndŵr left Wales and the Welsh in the

wilderness, but before the century was out the Welsh family of Tudor supplied England and Wales with a king when, in 1485, Harri Tudur became Henry VII. Welsh history and English history coincide politically following the Act of Union of 1536.

Socially that was never so because rural Wales was and is a poor country. The coal mines and steel industry of the south and the slate quarries of the north saw the exploitation of the Welsh by a new type of English overlord, although their effect on the people and the economy was similar to that of the barons of old. Ceredigion, having little mineral wealth (the blast furnace at Furnace – see Walk 2 – is the notable exception to this) was spared the worst excesses of this, and even had a measure of prosperity (see Walks 8, 11 and 12) because of the sheltered nature of its coast and the fertility of its soil.

The walks in this book explore all these periods in the history of Wales and Ceredigion. The interlocking nature of the county's history does not allow the walks to be easily assembled in chronological order. Therefore, rather than attempt such an ordering, they have been assembled from north to south.

Country Code
Enjoy the countryside and respect it's life and work.
Guard against all risk of fire.
Fasten all gates.
Keep your dogs under close control.
Keep to the public paths across farmland.
Use gates and stiles to cross fences, hedges and walls.
Leave livestock, crops and machinery alone.
Take your litter home.
Help to keep all water clean.
Protect wildlife, plants and trees.
Take special care on country roads.
Mak no unnecessary noise.

Welsh Place Names

Place names can be a fascinating study in their own right, indicating geographical features, patterns of former land ownership, forgotten buildings or former trades. However, the current place name may be far removed from the original name particularly where there is an anglicised form of an old Welsh name e.g. Pembroke is derived from Pen Fro, the Welsh for Land's End. Welsh place names are particularly expressive of geography, and can be highly poetic e.g. Pwll Deri, *pool of the oak trees*. Some of the more common names are listed below:

Aber – river mouth, estuary
Afon – river
Allt – wood, hill, slope
Bach/Fach – little
Bedd – grave
Bryn – hill
Bwlch – pass
Caer(au) – fort(s)
Canol – middle, centre
Capel – chapel
Carn – cairn
Carreg, pl. cerrig – rock, stone
Castell – castle
Cemais – river bend
Cleddau – sword
Coch – red
Coed – wood
Coetan – quoit
Cors – bog, marsh
Craig – rock, cliff
Crib – ridge
Croes – cross
Cromlech(au) – burial mound(s)
Cwm – valley

Cyhoeddus – public
Dan – under
Dau – two
Deri – oak
Dinas – hill fort
Dôl – meadow
Du, Ddu – black
Dŵr – water
Dyffryn – valley
Efail – smithy
Eglwys – church
Ffordd – road
Ffos – ditch, dyke
Ffynnon – spring, well
Gain – fair, fine, elegant
Garn – cairn
Gelli – grove
Glan – river bank
Gors – bog, marsh
Gwastad – level, flat
Gwaun – moor, meadow
Gwyn – white
Gwynt – wind
Hafod – summer dwelling

Cwrw – beer
Hendre – winter dwelling
Isaf – lower
Llan – church
Llannerch – clearing, glade
Llyn – lake
Llwybr – path/track
Llwyd – grey
Maen – rock/stone
Maes – field
Mawr/Fawr – great, big
Melin – mill
Melyn – yellow
Moel/Foel – bare topped hill
Morfa – marsh
Mynach – monk
Mynachlog – monastery
Mynydd – mountain
Nant – brook, stream
Newydd – new
Nos – night
Ogof – cave

Hen – old
Parc – field, park
Pen – head, top
Penrhyn – promontory, headland
Pentre – village
Plas – hall
Pont – bridge
Porth – harbour
Pwll – pool
Rhiw – hill
Rhos – moorland
Rhyd – ford
Sych – dry
Tafarn – inn
Traeth – beach
Tref – town, hamlet
Tŷ – house
Uchaf – upper
Y, Yr – the
Yn – in
Ynys – island
Ysgol – school

A few notes on pronunciation may help:

c – k (hard)
ch – as in lo*ch*
dd – th as in *th*at
f – v
ff – f
g – g (hard)
ll – (pronounce l, keep tongue in position at roof of mouth, and hiss!
the – th as in *th*ink
There are 7 vowels, a,e,i,o,u,w and y. Pronunciation may be long or short.

w may be as in pool, or pull e.g. *cwm* (coom) – valley
y may be as in fun, or pin e.g. *y,yr*, (u,ur) – the, *dyffryn* (dufrin)
– valley.

Many Welsh words change their pronunciation and spelling under certain circumstances e.g. the initial consonant of many words may soften: b to f, c to g, m to f, p to b etc. Common examples of mutations are *bach* (little) to *fach*; *mawr* (big) to *fawr*, *porth* (harbour) to *borth*. Such mutations can make tracing words through a dictionary a little problematic for the unitiated!

Tourist Information Centres
(* – open throughout the year. The remainder are open Easter-September. In general, when open, the offices are open daily, 10am-5.30pm)

Aberaeron, The Quay *	01545 570602
Aberystwyth, Terrace Road *	01970 612125
Aberteifi, Theatr Mwldan, Bath House Road *	01239 613230
Borth, Cambrian Terrace	01970 871174
Newcastle Emlyn, Market Hall	01239 711333
New Quay, Church Street	01545 560865
Tregaron, The Square	01974 298144

Weather and Transport Services
The Weathercall service offers 24-hour and 7-day forecasts by dialling:

24-hour	0891 300 114
7-day	0891 505 314

In addition, there is a 'faxback' forecast available by dialling 0891 333111, then code 716.

Ceredigion County Council publishes a booklet of all bus and train services in the county. This booklet is available free of charge at Tourist Information Offices.

The Valley of Afon Hyddgen, Pumlumon

OS Maps:	Landranger Sheet 135 (Aberystwyth and Machynlleth)
	Explorer Sheet 213 (Aberystwyth and Cwm Rheidol)
Start:	Grid Reference 774 879
Access:	To reach the start take the mountain road from Ponterwyd on the A44 east of Aberystwyth to Tal-y-bont on the A487 north of Aberystwyth. The road rises along the western flank of Pumlumon to reach the Nant y Moch Reservoir. Just before the reservoir, a road (a No-Through Road) goes off right to the Maesnant Outdoor Pursuits Centre. No buses run closer than Ponterwyd.
Parking:	The road is unfenced: park beside it close to Maesnant. Please park sensibly.
Grade:	Moderate. Though the walk is short and out-and-back so there is little chance of getting lost, the latter section cover rough, trackless moorland.

Points of Interest:

1. Pumlumon is an under-rated and much maligned area. In the mid-19th century the traveller WF Peacock came this way, finding 'bogland; uncertain sponge, with black pitchy water . . . dark herbage thrives and its complexion is just about as ghastly and healthless as you can imagine'. He was, he claimed, fortunate to escape the range alive. The man who ventured on it alone was 'no better than a fool. He has one chance of returning in safety; he has ninety-nine chances of being seen no more in

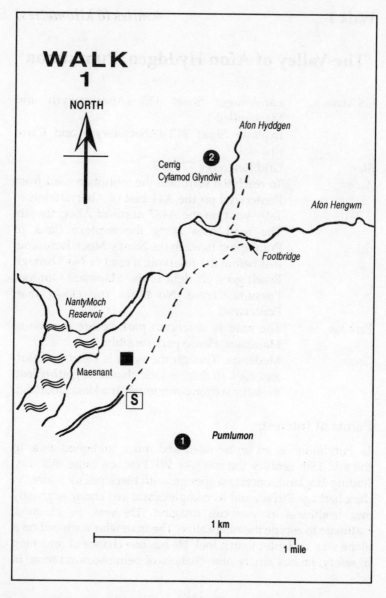

WALK 1

NORTH

Afon Hyddgen

2 Cerrig
Cyfamod Glyndŵr

Afon Hengwm

Footbridge

NantyMoch
Reservoir

Maesnant

S

1 Pumlumon

1 km

1 mile

life'. A later writer described Pumlumon as 'a sodden weariness' and even Thomas Pennant, a much-travelled man who, it might be imagined, was little bothered by minor discomforts, said that he had been 'dissuaded from making it a visit, being informed that it was an uninteresting object, the base most extensive, the top boggy and the view over a dreary and almost uninhabited country'. Ironically, given the obsession with Pumlumon's bogs, it is also claimed that after a hot day on Pumlumon, during which he and a companion were parched because of the lack of streams and standing water, Samuel Taylor Coleridge thought of the line 'water, water, everywhere. Nor any drop to drink' for his *Rime of the Ancient Mariner*.

In reality, Pumlumon is wonderful walking country, its high peaks (Pen Pumlumon Fawr and Pen Pumlumon Arwystli) standing close to the sources of the rivers Wye and Severn which are known here as Afonydd Gwy and Hafren. The first half is derived, perhaps, from *pump* meaning five. Five what? The most usual explanation is five rivers – the Severn, the Wye, the Rheidol and two others. But why only two others since there are many? Pumlumon is the mother of rivers, and all lists differ. Perhaps, then, it is five peaks, five summits? Again it is difficult; Pumlumon is all high and wild and, while there are distinct summits, it is not easy to see five rather than four or six. The renowned Welsh place-names expert, Bedwyr Lewis Jones, offered a further light on Pumlumon:

'The meaning of llumon is 'chimney', according to Sir Ifor. It can be translated as chimney pot also, and may be a used figuratively to describe a chimney-pot shaped mountain. Sir Ifor adds that he heard that five chimney-pot shaped peaks – that is, five *llumon* – in the chain of mountains called *Pumlumon.*'

2. Following the Norman invasion of England the Norman kings left the Welsh to themselves, the conquest of this appendage to their new realm not being a priority. But

recognising the hostility of Wales to its large neighbour and the fighting qualities of the Welsh, the Norman kings decided to create a barrier between Wales and England. To do this the kings created the Marcher Lords. These were Norman lords who owned land on the *march*, or border, between the countries. The eastern boundary of the marcher lords' lands were defined, as were the boundaries between the lordships, but the western borders were of the lords' own choosing – they could grab as much Welsh land as they thought they could hold. Such a system was bound to create antagonism, and the years of conflict which followed were answered by a consistent attitude by the Norman (eventually English) kings: they attacked the Welsh, killing and looting, and then passed anti-Welsh legislation which only fuelled Welsh bitterness. In 1399 those Welsh who were loyal to the English crown, and there were many, particularly close to the border, were appalled when Henry Bolingbroke usurped, as they saw it, the crown of Richard II (a relatively pro-Welsh king), particularly as the betrayal which led to Richard's capture was enacted in Wales, at Fflint Castle.

In the same year that Bolingbroke became Henry IV, Lord Reginald Grey of Rhuthun exercised his right, as he saw it, as a marcher lord by stealing some land from his Welsh neighbour. That neighbour was Owain Glyndŵr, a high-born Welshman who could trace his lineage to the royal houses of Gwynedd, Powys and Deheubarth. But times had changed since the conquest and instead of attacking Grey and seizing his rightful property, Glyndŵr took the lord to court, assured of success. The court found against him and, to add insult to injustice, stated that they had found for the English lord because 'what care we for barefoot Welsh dogs'.

Victory in the legal battle emboldened Grey – perhaps he could have even more of Glyndŵr's land. In 1400 his chance came. Henry IV was to campaign in Scotland and sent a message to Glyndŵr to join him. As a royal subject Glyndŵr was bound to attend and, as one who had a knowledge of Scotland from a previous campaign under King Richard, he would have been a useful asset. But Henry's message to Glyndŵr was entrusted to Lord Grey and he, for his own ends, failed to pass it on. When Henry's army was humiliated, the king looked around for persons to blame. One of those, he decided, was Owain Glyndŵr and he gave Grey permission to seize his lands. Grey's attempt to seize Glyndŵr too failed, the Welshman escaping into the hills. From there, with a small band of retainers, Glyndŵr attacked Rhuthun and several other marcher towns. In response Henry IV raised an army and marched on Wales. He executed captured rebels, looted and burned a few villages and offered an amnesty to the remaining rebels. Most of them accepted. Glyndŵr's rebellion was, it seemed, over. By 1401 Glyndŵr was a fugitive, holed up in Pumlumon's Hyddgen valley.

Many years before, Henry I had brought Flemish weavers and other craftsmen from the continent and set them up in south-west Wales so as to destabalize the political situation in the area. The newcomers had grown prosperous, chiefly occupying the southern part of the old county of Pembrokeshire, but also moving into parts of Ceredigion and Carmarthenshire. Civil unrest now threatened their prosperity and their well-ordered lives, and their allegiance was very much to the English King. Fearing that Glyndŵr might start a civil war, they raised an army of 1,500 men and marched north towards Pumlumon. Their plan was to catch Glyndŵr unaware in his secret hideout and to put an end to the rebellion before it had a chance to grow. It was a flawed plan: Glyndŵr would have been best left alone, a lonely rebel who might possibly have been forgotten in a year or two. But the Flemings could not see that and when, by luck, good planning or appalling slackness on the part of Glyndŵr's men, they were able to encircle and surprise the Welsh, their plan seemed to have come to excellent fruition. They outnumbered the Welsh by four to one and poured in on them. A contemporary account notes that: 'they hemmed him (Glyndŵr) in on all sides so that he could not possibly get off without fighting at a great disadvantage. He and his men fought manfully a great while, in their own defence, against them. Finding themselves surrounded and hard put to, they resolved at length to make their way through or perish in the attempt: so, falling on furiously, with courage whetted with despair they put the enemy, after a sharp dispute, to confusion; and they pursued so eagerly their advantage, that they bade them give ground, and in the end to fly outright, leaving 200 of their men dead on the spot of the engagement'.

It was a great, and unlikely, victory and the effect on the Welsh was both immediate and overwhelming: a new hero was created. As the account of the battle continues: 'This victory rendered Owain considerable renown and was the means to bring many to his side, that his number was greatly increased'.

At the site of the battle the Welsh placed two dazzling white calcite blocks, *Cerrig Cyfamod Glyndŵr* (the covenant stones of Owain Glyndŵr), not only to commemorate the victory and also as a symbol of their pledge of allegiance to their new prince.

Walk Directions   [-] denotes Point of Interest

1. Continue along the road from your starting point. At the gate, ignore the track bearing left to Maesnant, continuing along the stony track ahead, with the steep ground of Fainc Ddu to the right. Beyond this is the sweep of Pumlumon Fach and, beyond, the high peaks of Pumlumon Fawr. [1]

2. Follow the track to another gate, beyond which there is a footbridge over Afon Hengwm. To the right a footpath follows this pretty river reaching a pair of attractive waterfalls. Our route crosses the bridge, bearing left to reach Afon Hyddgen and turning north to follow it.

3. Across the stream is the site of the battle[2], the covenant stones being visible. A footpath crosses Afon Hyddgen close to

its confluence with Afon Hengwm, but then continues west below Banc Llechwedd-mawr, eventually reaching the northern shore of the Nant y Moch Reservoir. Unfortunately it does not pass the stones, which lie on private land. On the eastern side of Afon Hyddgen, the right of way can be followed through a windswept, bleak, yet beautiful landscape.

4. To return, reverse the outward journey back to the start.

Refreshments

None. This is a remote walk: all refreshments must be brought by the walker.

WALK 2

NORTH

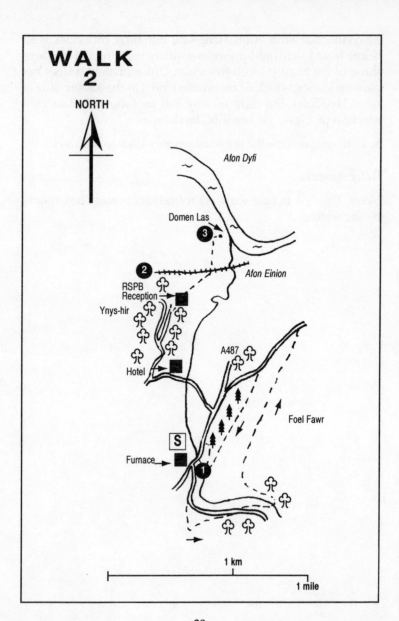

Afon Dyfi

Domen Las
3

2
Afon Einion

RSPB
Reception →

Ynys-hir

Hotel

A487

Foel Fawr

S

Furnace →

1

| 1 km |
| 1 mile |

Walk 2   *3½ miles (5.5 kilometres), but with an*
                  extension to 6½ miles (10.5 kilometres)

Ffwrnais (Furnace)

OS Maps:	Landranger Sheet 135 (Aberystwyth and Machynlleth)
	Outdoor Leisure Sheet 23 (Cadair Idris and Bala Lake/Llyn Tegid)
Start:	Furnace
Access:	Furnace lies on the main A487 which links Aberystwyth to Machynlleth. It is served by ArrivaCymru buses which link Aberystwyth, Machynlleth and Dolgellau.
Parking:	The CADW car park at Furnace.
Grade:	Moderate. Good paths but quite strenuous, particularly if the extension is walked.

Points of Interest:

1. During the 1750s the ironmaking company of Vernon, Kendall and Co, looking for fresh supplies of charcoal to fire their furnaces – it took at least 16 tons of wood to produce one ton of iron and the forests of northern England and southern Wales were soon denuded – came to north Ceredigion. Here at the hamlet now known as Furnace (Ffwrnais) they found what they were looking for. Afon Einion flowing swiftly down Cwm Einion could power water-wheels, the local forests could supply charcoal in plenty, and the nearby Afon Dyfi was navigable to shipping as far as Derwenlas: these ships could bring in ironstone and limestone for the furnace. By 1774 the Kendall family had acquired sole ownership of the furnace, adding it to their ironmaking interests in Scotland, Cumbria, Cheshire and Staffordshire. The building at Furnace is typical of its period. At

the western end was the furnace, a tapered cylinder that was charged at first floor level with iron ore, charcoal and limestone (as a flux) from the stone building set slightly further up the valley. The charging was by hand, probably a primitive wheelbarrow being tipped over the lip of the open-topped furnace – hot, smoky and very dangerous work. To the side of the building was a water-wheel which drove a shaft on which sat two cams which operated huge bellows, providing a continuous air blast to the base of the furnace. The closed bellows was re-opened by a counterweight. The molten iron from the furnace would have been tapped from the base, flowing into 'pigs' (moulds) formed in a sand tray. Although Afon Einion was a powerful stream its flow suffered seasonal variations, which were smoothed out by the building of a dam above the furnace, water from the pool formed behind it being taken through a leat to the wheel. Below the wheel, the water was discharged back into the stream.

The Kendall's furnace operated for about 50 years, transport costs probably hastening its end. The abandoned building was later converted into a sawmill: the water-wheel that is such a picturesque part of today's scene dates from this later usage. The site is now in the care of CADW and is one of the most interesting of its type and period in the whole country.

2. In terms of habitat, Ynys-hir is arguably the most diverse of all the Welsh reserves owned by the Royal Society for the Protection of Birds (RSPB). There is both broadleaf (much of it oak) and conifer woodland – the broadleaf areas are remnants of the woods that were managed by the charcoal makers who supplied Furnace – low-lying peat bog and saltmarsh at the tidal edge of the Dyfi. In the newer forests at the western edge of the reserve, there are freshwater pools, and the drainage ditches in the peat and forested areas provide yet another habitat. At the reception building – an entrance fee is payable for non-RSPB members, but as this is nominal and is used for the upkeep of the reserve no one can realistically complain – a

blackboard gives a list of uncommon species that have been seen recently. Giving a list of species visitors should see is fraught with danger, but the following are those which are relatively common. In the woodland there are redstarts, greater and lesser spotted woodpeckers, pied flycatchers, nuthatches and goldcrests, as well as more common species of tits, finches etc. Closer to the estuary there are reed, sedge and grasshopper warblers, while the waders include oystercatchers and curlew, both of which are year long residents. In winter, bar-tailed godwits are frequent residents, while greenshank, whimbrel and many more are visitors. The resident water birds include shelduck and red-breasted mergansers, but in winter these are joined by teal, pintail, goldeneye, wigeon and white-fronted geese. Of the birds of prey, the rarest are hen harrier and merlin. Peregrine falcons are often seen in winter.

The woodland has numerous boxes to attract nesting birds, while on the estuary there are several hides for viewing the waders and water birds.

3. At the northern end of the RSPB site is a heronry, one of the most important in Wales. During the nesting season, February to July, access to the area around the heronry is forbidden , but at other times visitors can reach the Domen Las Hide from where a fine section of Afon Dyfi is visible. The hide is named for Domen Las, the motte (mound) of a medieval castle that was probably built by Rhys ap Gruffudd in 1156. At that time Owain Gwynedd, ruler of the powerful house of Gwynedd, was making threats against independent, but vulnerable, Ceredigion. The castle, that was built on the border between the rival states, was a response to the threat. In the event the threat was just that, but the castle's existence was something the marcher lords saw as a threat to their own position, despite its remoteness from their lands. In 1158 Roger de Clare attacked the castle. He successfully took it, but holding it so far from Norman England was a different matter. Within twelve months Lord Rhys had retaken it. After that the castle disappears from the

historical record. What remains is a motte about 7m (23ft) high and some 10m (33m) in diameter across its flattened top. It is protected on three sides by deep ditches, on the fourth by the marshland of the Dyfi estuary. To the north-east are the remains of a rectangular area which may once have also been protected: perhaps it was the bailey of the castle.

Walk Directions   [-] denotes Point of Interest

1. From the car park, return to the A487. The old furnace building [1] is across the road. Cross the A487, with care, and follow the lane signed for Cwm Einion/Artists Valley. The lane climbs and then goes around a sharp left-hand bend. A short detour takes the signed path ahead here, following it to a crossing track. Turn left to savour a superb view of the Dyfi estuary with the Tarren range of hills as a backdrop to the North. The track now descends through fine woodland to regain the lane.

2. If you have not taken the short detour, continue along the lane for about 450m beyond the left bend to reach a signed, crossing path. The detour comes in on the right here, while the continuation turns left, descending through fine woodland to reach a footbridge over Afon Einion.

3. Follow the path beyond the bridge uphill to reach a lane. Cross this, following the signed path opposite, which climbs steadily to another fine viewpoint of the Dyfi estuary on the flank of Foel Fawr, the hill to the right.

4. Continue along the path which descends to reach a road close to a farm. Turn left along the road.

5. Those not walking the suggested extension to Ynys-hir – the walk can be made into two short walks as there is parking at the RSPB reception building – now turn left along a signed path. Follow this to reach a lane. Turn right, following the lane to reach the A487. Turn left, with care, for the short distance to the start.

6. To continue to Ynys-hir as an extension of the walk, ignore the signed path to the left in (5) above, following the lane to the A487. Turn left then cross, with care, to reach a turning on the right for the RSPB reserve and the Ynys-hir Hall Hotel. Follow this narrow and pretty lane past the entrance to the hotel, then turn right (as signed) where the lane continues to Ynys-hir Farm. The RSPB reception building is reached by taking the more rugged lane, as signed.

7. Walks of any length from 2-4 miles can be organised within the reserve, and all are worthwhile. To visit the Domen Las site (and the heronry) go around the reception building, with it on your left, and through a gate on to an enclosed lane. Turn right to reach another gate. Beyond this, go ahead where a track bears left. Cross the railway bridge (this is the Cambrian Coast line) and walk ahead for about 200m to reach a path on the right. This leads to Domen Las.

Refreshments

Limited to the garage in Furnace, but available on the A487 both north and south of the village, eg at Talybont, to the south. There are also limited refreshments at the RSPB building.

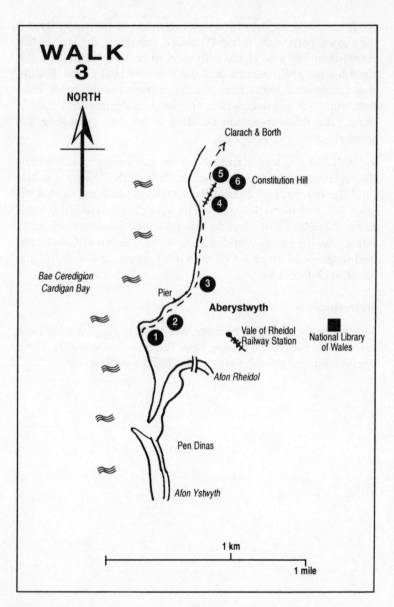

WALK
3

NORTH

Clarach & Borth

⑤ ⑥ Constitution Hill

④

Bae Ceredigion
Cardigan Bay

Pier

③

Aberystwyth

② Vale of Rheidol
① Railway Station

National Library
of Wales

Afon Rheidol

Pen Dinas

Afon Ystwyth

1 km

1 mile

Constitution Hill, Aberystwyth

OS Maps:	Landranger Sheet 135 (Aberystwyth and Machynlleth)
	Explorer Sheet 213 (Aberystwyth and Cwm Rheidol)
Start:	Aberystwyth Castle
Access:	Aberystwyth is the major town of Ceredigion, served by the A487, A44, A4120 and A485 main roads, and also by train.
Parking:	There are numerous options in the town. Parking is available close to the castle, as well as at the nearby harbour.
Grade:	Easy. Very straightforward town walking and good paths on the hill.

Points of Interest:

1. The first castle at Aberystwyth was a Norman motte and bailey built by Gilbert de Strongbow in about 1109, an early incursion of a Norman baron into Wales securing the headland close to Llanbadarn, one of the spiritual centres of Wales. Gilbert presumably did not hold the castle long for it was in the hands of Cadwaladr, a son of Gruffudd ap Cynan, in 1143 when in a petty dispute with Anarawd, son of Gruffudd ap Rhys of Deheubarth, he killed Anarawd. At the time Anarawd was set to marry one of the daughters of Owain Gwynedd. Owain was Cadwaladr's brother and ruler of Gwynedd, the marriage allowing him to expand his sphere of influence to include Deheubarth and so, hopefully and eventually, to unify Wales against the Normans. Faced with a choice between supporting his brother or continuing with his political ends, Owain chose

the latter, forcing his brother into exile. One of his first acts was to take Cadwaladr's main castle, here at Aberystwyth.

The first castle would have been of wood, with defensive earthworks, but as part of Edward I's 'Ring of Stone' built after his campaigns of the late 13th century, that early structure was replaced with one in stone. As with all of Edward's castles, Aberystwyth could be supplied by sea – the Welsh could lay siege, but with a sea-gate the castle could hold out indefinitely.

Edward's castle remained a Norman stronghold for over a century until it was captured by the Welsh during the struggles of Owain Glyndŵr. In 1404 Glyndŵr controlled almost all of Wales, his position being so secure that he could turn his attention to the great castles. In quick succession Harlech, Cricieth and Aberystwyth were taken by his forces. Although he used Harlech as his main stronghold Aberystwyth was important, standing at the border between the north, which would always follow him, and the south which, historically, had been under Norman rule and so needed to be watched. By 1407 Owain's position was in decline and his forces in retreat. During the summer Prince Henry – the Monmouth-born son of Henry IV, a young man who would become the legendary Henry V – arrived at the castle walls with an army and the newest weapon in the king's armoury, cannons. There were seven cannons in all, including a $4^{1}/_{2}$ ton monster called the King's Gonne and another called, with the gallows humour of the military, The Messenger. With the cannon came five hundredweight of powder, nine hundredweight of saltpetre and three hundredweight of sulphur. The castle garrison, used to siege engines but never having seen a cannon, were terrified by the initial bombardment. But equally fearful were the cannoniers: medieval cannon were notoriously dangerous and one at the siege exploded killing everyone close to it.

But, despite the cannon, the castle held out. By September both sides were weary, and the castle commander, Rhys Ddu, took advantage of this to offer Prince Henry a deal. He suggested a truce until 24 October at which point fighting would resume for a week. If by 1 November the castle had not been relieved Rhys would surrender it. Prince Henry accepted, a treaty was signed and the Prince's army retreated to Strata Florida for a rest. Owain Glyndŵr took his chance to resupply and reinforce the castle.

The understandably annoyed Prince Henry returned, laying siege through a savage winter that saw snow blanket the whole of Wales from Christmas until March. With dwindling supplies the castle garrison waited for the thaw and relief, but Owain was not in a position to resupply by sea and his tenuous hold on the countryside meant he could not resupply by land either. By late 1408 the situation was hopeless and the castle surrendered.

Much later the castle was used as a mint with silver from local lead mines being used for the coinage, but the building was then abandoned to the elements. Today only the remains of a few walls and one round tower remain.

2. During his period of power Owain held a parliament at Machynlleth, to the north of Aberystwyth, at which he outlined his vision of a Wales free of English domination. One of his aims was to create a university so that an educated generation of the Welsh could organise the country's own affairs. It is ironic, therefore, that within a few seconds walk from the castle that was one of Glyndŵr's main strongholds, there is a college of the University of Wales. In the 1860s Thomas Savin, builder of the Cambrian Coast railway line, built a hotel at Aberystwyth with the idea of selling a package from London's Euston which included return rail fare and nights at a quality hotel. The venture failed and in 1870 the derelict hotel was bought by a group of Welshman with the intention of creating a new college of the University of Wales. The new college opened in 1872 with just 26 students. For 10 years the college was maintained by voluntary fund raising, but then the Government was persuaded to grant finance. Since then the college has expanded, both in terms of buildings and student numbers, and

in reputation: its faculty of agriculture and plant biology is world renowned.

Many of the College's buildings lie on Penglais Hill up which the A487 exits Aberystwyth (though several of the student halls of residence occupy old hotels on the sea front). One of the most impressive buildings on the hill houses the National Library of Wales, established by a charter of Edward VII in 1907. The idea was put forward in 1873 but, as with many things in and concerning Wales, it took several decades of campaigning for the idea to come to fruition. The university idea took 470 years. Under the copyright Act of 1911 the Library is entitled to a copy of all books, pamphlets, maps etc published in the United Kingdom. The library has the first book to be published in Welsh and the first to have been published in Wales, as well as many priceless medieval manuscripts.

3. From the southern end of the sea-front promenade, Aberystwyth reveals itself as the archetypal Victorian sea-side resort; the beach to the left just beyond the pier, and to the right an array of elegant houses, many of them once hotels. Once known as the 'Brighton of Wales' (which always comes across like a back-handed compliment) the town claimed to be the possessor of many sunshine and temperature records for Britain, and to have the most temperate winters of any British resort. The town is now home to the largest Arts Centre in Wales and the Ceredigion Museum (next to the Tourist Information Office in Terrace Road), which explores the history of the county. The museum is housed in a former theatre and has been described as 'probably the most beautiful museum in Britain'.

4. The Electric Cliff Railway was built in 1896 by George Croydon Marks, who was also partly responsible for the pier at the other end of the sea front. Engineered to allow holidaymakers to enjoy the view and to take a constitution at the top of the hill, the funicular was originally powered by gravity, a water tank on the descending train being filled so that

its weight hauled the ascending train up. At the bottom the tank was emptied into the sea. Only later were the electric motors that give the railway its name installed. The track is 237m (778ft) long, the longest in Britain. The funicular runs only during the holiday season.

5. Constitution Hill is named for the walks taken by Victorian seasiders as part of their Aberystwyth holiday or rest cure. The walkers were also entertained by a standard series of amusements in 'Luna Park' – bandstand, ballroom, camera obscura (see below) and even an early roller coaster.

The view from the hill is impressive and explains the importance of Aberystwyth's site. Between the hill and Pen Dinas to the south is a small, but well-sheltered, bay into which Afon Ystwyth flows, a naturally strategic site. Pen Dinas is topped by an Iron Age hill-fort in which stands the Wellington Monument, erected in 1852 to commemorate the Iron Duke's victory at Waterloo in 1815.

6. The Camera Obscura was built in Victorian times for the delight and amusement of the holidaymakers. The original version was housed a short distance from the present building, which was erected in 1985 with a new 14 inch (35 cm) lens (then the biggest in the world). Using a mirror at the top of the building and the lens a view of the surrounding countryside is projected on to the viewing table. It is said that a clear image of 2,500 square kilometres (1,000 square miles) of country surrounding Aberystwyth can be seen in good weather. Close to the camera obscura, the Summerhouse Tearooms were built at about the same time as the funicular, making them (probably) the oldest cafe in town.

Walk Directions   [-] denotes Point of Interest

1. From the castle [1] head towards the town, soon passing the administrative buildings of the University College [2] to the right. The pier is soon reached. It was built in 1864, but

refurbished in 1896 and again in 1922. It is 213m (700ft) long. From close to the pier there is an impressive view of Aberystwyth's seafront [3].

2. Continue along the seafront, either by taking the wide pavement above the beach or by walking along the beach itself. At the far end of the seafront is the lower station of the cliff railway [4]. There is now a choice: either take the railway or climb the steep path to the top of Constitution Hill [5].

3. The path – or, rather, one of the paths as there is quite a complex, just keep going up – crosses the railway a couple of times, eventually reaching the top station with its gift shop etc. Close by is the Camera Obscura [6].

4. From the summit of Constitution Hill the walk can be extended to any length by following the cliff path northwards to Clarach, or even on to Borth (about 6 miles – 9.5 kilometres). Alternatively, return to the castle by detouring through the town.

Refreshments

Every taste and pocket is catered for in Aberystwyth.

Pontarfynach (Devil's Bridge) and Cwm Rheidol

OS Maps:	Landranger Sheet 135 (Aberystwyth and Machynlleth)
	Explorer Sheet 213 (Aberystwyth and Cwm Rheidol)
Start:	Pontarfynach (Devil's Bridge)
Access:	Pontarfynach (Devil's Bridge) lies on the A4120, the road which rises through Cwm Rheidol from Aberystwyth to Ponterwyd, where it links with the A44. Pontarfynach can also be reached from Aberystwyth by the Vale of Rheidol railway and several buses.
Parking:	There is a car park close to the famous falls, and at the Vale of Rheidol railway terminus.
Grade:	Difficult. Though short, the walk has one sharp climb (unless the railway option is used).

Ideally a walk around the *Devil's Bridge* falls would be offered, but crossing points of Afon Rheidol are limited, and all such walks involve a section of main road. This walk minimises road walking, and also has an option of using the Vale of Rheidol Railway so as to eliminate roads altogether.

Points of Interest:

1. Despite being associated with beautiful Cwm Rheidol the triple bridges of Devil's Bridge do not actually cross Afon Rheidol. The river below is the Afon Mynach, the monk's river, named for the monks of the abbey at Strata Florida who owned sheep grazing land in the area. It was the monks who built the

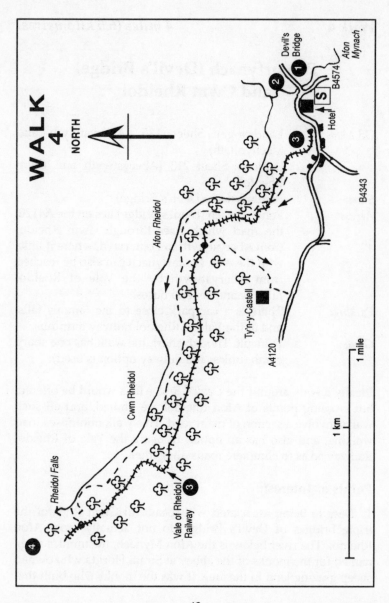

WALK
4
NORTH

Devil's Bridge
Afon Mynach
B4574
S
Hotel
B4343

Afon Rheidol

Cwm Rheidol

Ty'n-y-Castell
A4120

Rheidol Falls

Vale of Rheidol
Railway

1 mile
1 km

first bridge – the lower one of course! – in 1087 and it was called Pontarfynach (the Monk's Bridge), which is still the Welsh name for the hamlet. The English name is a translation of Pont-y-gwr-drwg, literally the bridge of the Evil One, the name deriving from a legend about the method of construction of the first bridge. The legend concerns Marged, an old woman who lived alone close to the edge of the ravine making a living by selling the milk of Malen, her only cow. One morning, after a night of torrential rain, Marged went out to milk Malen but discovered that before the rain had started the cow had crossed the stream, and was now marooned on the far side by a raging torrent. Marged was in despair – if she did not milk Malen not only would there be no milk to sell but the cow would also suffer. What would happen to Marged if the cow died? Marged wrung her hands and shouted loudly that she would give anything for a bridge to cross the stream. To her astonishment a voice answered that he would build her a bridge and, looking across the ravine, she saw a figure in the distinctive white habit and cowl of a Strata Florida monk. Marged could not see his face, and the cowl seemed oddly shaped, but so desperate was she that the details did not really register. Neither did the fact that she could clearly hear the stranger over the rush of the water below. Marged asked how long the bridge would take and the stranger replied about an hour, but that she must not watch the work. She agreed, hurrying back to her cottage so quickly that she failed to notice the significance of the stranger's final remark, that he must be allowed to take the first living thing which crossed the bridge.

After an hour of anxious waiting Marged returned to find the bridge in place, but as she started to cross she saw that the monk's cowl had slipped slightly, revealing the reason for the curious shape – the stranger had horns, it was the Devil in disguise. Now Marged recalled his final sentence and realised that she would forfeit her soul if she crossed. She hesitated and stared at the bridge. The impatient Devil asked her what the problem was and she replied that the bridge did not look secure, in fact it did not seem strong enough to bear the weight of the crust of bread she was carrying, a morsel from her breakfast. The exasperated Devil said that to test the bridge she should throw the crust on to it, but Marged threw the crust right across the bridge and her dog immediately scampered after it, becoming the first living thing to cross. The furious Devil disappeared in a cloud of sulphurous smoke, but the bridge remained intact allowing Marged to be re-united with Malen and her dog.

The triple bridges are an object lesson in the advance of bridge building techniques. As span lengths could be increased the bridges moved nearer to the top of the ravine.

2. Beneath the bridges are the Mynach Falls and the Devil's Punchbowl, superb natural creations, access to which is strictly controlled and by payment only. Most walkers will have mixed feelings about this; on the debit side, how can anyone charge for such a natural phenomenon? On the other hand we live in a country where, rightly or wrongly, all land is privately owned (even common and open-access land) and the owners do maintain the paths and steps, for the benefit of everyone.

Glimpses of the beauty spots can be obtained from the bridge and road edges, but to explore them thoroughly the site must be visited. It is very worthwhile – this really is a very beautiful gorge, one of the best natural scenes in Ceredigion if not the whole of Wales. The Punchbowl lies on the southern side of the bridges, a smooth hollow in the bed rock of the stream caused by millennia of scouring by pebbles carried by the rushing water. To the north of the bridge are the falls and some marvellous woodland. To experience the best of them it is necessary to descend almost 100m (300ft) to the river, reaching a point close to the confluence of Afon Mynach and Afon Rheidol.

It almost seems so self-evident that this site is beautiful that it comes as a surprise to find that George Barrow, that intrepid mid-19th century traveller whose book *Wild Wales* has become such a classic, did not share the opinion. Borrow stayed at the Hafod Arms Hotel, the 'immense lofty cottage with projecting eaves' which still stands. Borrow viewed the scene below the bridges with the awe-struck horror that seemed to be the requirement of visitors of the period. The Punchbowl was 'a frightful cavity (where) the waters . . . whirl, boil and hiss in a horrid pot or cauldron . . . in a manner truly tremendous'. The waters then escape through 'a gloomy volcanic slit'. Borrow suggested that, after seeing the Punchbowl (which he called by the local name of Twll yn y Graig) and the 'spectral, shadowy Devil's Bridge', you should 'repair to your inn, and have no more sight-seeing that day, for you have seen enough!' Neither could he come to terms with the falls themselves which were 'thundering beside you; foam, foam, foam is flying all about you; the basin . . . is boiling frightfully below you', together with 'rocks . . . frowning terribly on you' and 'forest trees, dank and wet with spray and mist'. It would be interesting to find out if Borrow really did find it so bad, or whether his intended audience coloured his perception. For the modern walker it is all of these horrid, frightful things that are so attractive.

Borrow does not mention the legend of Marged and the Devil, but he does mention a story centred on a cave, now no longer visible as such, at the base of the falls. Here, he says, lived the Plant de Bat, or children of Bat, a local man. They, two boys and a girl, were notorious locally as petty thieves. One day they killed a gentleman while robbing him, and his friends sought them out, destroying the cave so they could no longer use it. The boys were hanged and the girl burnt at the stake.

3. The Vale of Rheidol Railway opened in 1902, chiefly to transport the ore from the lead mines of Cwm Rheidol, which were dotted along the upper valley from Aber-ffrwd to Pontarfynach, though the line also carried timber and passengers. The awkward terrain, and the usual desire to save money, meant that a narrow gauge track was laid. The last of the

mines closed around the time of the 1914-18 War after which the line became one of the major tourist attractions of Aberystwyth, coaches from Pontarfynach taking visitors to see Pumlumon. The line was taken over by Great Western Railways in 1922 and was the last steam service to be operated by British Rail. In 1989 it was taken over by the Brecon Mountain Railway Co. and is now operated as one of the 'Great Little Trains of Wales'. The journey from Devil's Bridge to Aberystwyth (or vice versa) takes an hour.

4. Just beyond the pretty Rheidol Falls the valley has been flooded to create the Cwm Rheidol Reservoir. At its head, close to the Falls, is a hydro-electric power station operated by PowerGen. The station and its fish farm can be visited, and there is also an information centre.

Walk Directions   [-] denotes Point of Interest

1. From Pontarfynach (Devil's Bridge) [1] and the entrance to the natural scenery of Afon Mynach [2], follow the A4120, with care, past the Hafod Arms Hotel.

2. Continue past the terminus of the Vale of Rheidol railway [3] and through the hamlet of Devil's Bridge/Pontarfynach. Walk past two houses to the right, Llys Maeth and Fronhaul, turning right beyond on the latter along a path which heads north, soon reaching woodland beside the railway.

3. The path soon reaches the railway. Cross, with care, and continue, now walking close to the line. Eventually the path drops away from the line, falling steeply as it sweeps in a gentle leftward curve towards Afon Rheidol. The mixed, but chiefly conifer, wood, here is superb and excellent for woodland birds.

4. Ignore a path going off to the right (for Pont Bren Plwca, over Afon Rheidol) continuing to reach a T-junction of paths.

5. There is a choice here. Turning right allows a clear path to be

followed to the Rheidol Falls [4] and the nearby railway station. From there the train can be taken back to Pontarfynach. This has the advantage of a ride on the train, a relaxing return, and the avoidance of the short section of walking on the A4120. The disadvantage, of course, is the need to time your arrival to a train's departure.

6. To return by foot, turn left, following the path (it is actually a bridleway) across the railway again (close to the Rhiwfren Station). Beyond, the path continues through woodland, then beside fences to Ty'n-y-Castell Farm. Now take the farm access lane to reach the A4120.

7. Turn left and follow the road, with care, back to Pontarfynach.

Refreshments

There are several possibilities at Pontarfynach.

WALK
5a

NORTH

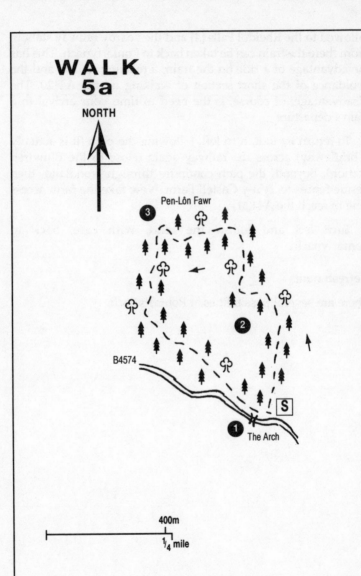

Pen-Lôn Fawr

❸

❷

B4574

S

❶ The Arch

400m
¼ mile

Walk 5

a) The Arch Trail *1½ miles (2.5 kilometres)*
b) The Hafod Trail *2 miles (3 kilometres)*
c) Cwmystwyth *1½ miles (2.5 kilometres)*

OS Maps: Landranger Sheet 135 (Aberystwyth and
              Machynlleth)
              Explorer Sheet 213 (Aberystwyth and Cwm
              Rheidol)

These three short walks close to Pontarfynach explore north
Ceredigion's mining history, as well as the work of an early
'green' pioneer.

Walk 5a
Start: The Forestry Commission car park/picnic site
             at Grid Reference 765 755, just beyond The Arch.
Access: The car park lies beside the B4574 which heads
             south from Pontarfynach, eventually reaching
             Pont-rhyd-y-groes. There is no public transport
             to the site. (There is a bus from Pontarfynach to
             Pont-rhyd-y-groes (J Alwyn Evans bus 538), but
             this takes the direct route.)
Grade: Moderate. Though short, the route involves
             some climbing.

Walk 5b
Start: The Forestry Commission car park/picnic site
             at Hafod, at Grid Reference 765 736.
Access: This car park also lies beside the B4574 about 3
             miles (5 kilometres) to the south of The Arch.
             There is no public transport to the site.
Grade: Easy. There is some climbing, but the ascents
             are gentle.

Walk 5c

Start: At Grid Reference 803 745, at the western end of the mining site.

Access: On its way from Pontarfynach to Pont-rhyd-y-groes, between The Arch and Hafod car parks, the B4574 makes a very sharp right bend. At the crown of this, a road goes off left (eastwards). Take this to reach the mine sites close to Afon Ystwyth. The Ceredigion Postbus passes the site on its way from Aberystwyth to Llangurig.

Parking: Roadside parking is easily organised at the site.

Grade: Easy. Level walking beside the road.

Walk 5a
Points of Interest:

1. The Arch was erected in 1810 by Thomas Johnes of Hafod to celebrate the Golden Jubilee of George III's accession to the throne. Johnes found this section of his estate to have been spoiled by 'great digging for trade, the melting wherof hath destroid the wooddes that sumtime grew plentifulli thereabout'. The trade Johnes spoke of was the local mining, the 'melting' presumably being the need for charcoal in the smelting process. Johnes obviously knew the centre of the mining was in Cwmystwyth, noting that 'in Comentswith . . . the wood is sore wastith'. In an endeavour to rectify the situation Johnes planted over five million trees between 1796 and 1813, much of the planting was of larch, but it also included many acorns. This was marvellously far-sighted, demonstrating Johnes's concern for the environment because he could not have hoped to see the oaks in his lifetime.

2. The Forestry Commission have continued Johnes' work, though the choice of Japanese larch, lodgepole pine and sitka spruce is not to everyone's taste. However, broadleaves have been planted in the sheltered areas, the species including beech,

rowan, willow and western hemlock. Some of Johnes' oaks and beech – or, perhaps, their offspring – survive too, magnificent trees, tall and well spread. Within the woodland, look out for tits and finches, as well as rarer species such as the redpoll. Lucky walkers may also catch a glimpse of a jay, the most colourful of the crow family, while overhead buzzards (and even red kites) may be seen.

3. The Pen-lan Fawr viewpoint is only 440m (1,450ft) above sea level, but offers a wonderful view towards Aberystwyth and north towards Pumlumon and Cadair Idris.

Walk Directions   [-] denotes Point of Interest

1. From the start close to The Arch [1], follow the numbered red waymarkers north into the woodland [2].

2. At Waymarker 2, white and yellow shortcuts branch off to the left. Ignore these as the red route must be followed to reach the viewpoint [3] at Waymarker 6. The yellow route rejoins at Waymarker 8, but now no longer offers a shortcut: continue along the red route to regain the start.

Walk 5b
Points of Interest:

1. The church glimpsed through the trees is Eglwys Newydd. The first church here was built in 1620 by William Herbert, an early owner of the Hafod estate, but it was rebuilt by Thomas Johnes in the early years of the 19th century to a design by James Wyatt, one of the leading architects of the day. As with the mansion, the church was destroyed by fire, though not until 1932, a century after Johnes' death. It was subsequently rebuilt in an interesting style, the body late Norman, the crenellated tower extremely fanciful. Thomas Johnes and his daughter Mariamne, are buried in the chancel.

2. At Hafod Thomas Johnes (1748-1816) landscaped the estate,

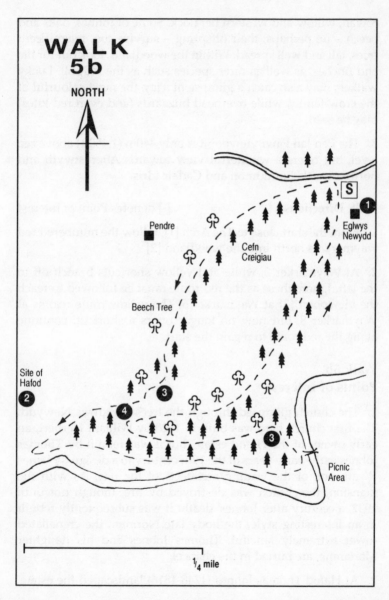

WALK
5b

NORTH

Pendre

Cefn
Creigiau

Beech Tree

Eglwys
Newydd

S

1

Site of
Hafod

2

3

4

3

Picnic
Area

¼ mile

developing a series of paths which obtained the best views of the natural scenery of this section of the Ystwyth Valley. He also built a marvellous Gothic mansion, to the west of the walk, but this was destroyed by fire in 1807. Johnes had it rebuilt in similar style. Sadly, at the end of his life Johnes was ruined financially and had to sell Hafod, moving to Devon, though he and his only daughter were buried at Eglwys Newydd. After his death the new owner, Anthony Salvin, had the mansion extended in fine Italianate style. Unfortunately the house was stripped of all its valuables, including the roof timbers, in 1938 and left ruinous. Plans by the Forestry Commission to salvage what remained were thwarted by the extremely dangerous condition of the ruin and, in 1958, it was demolished.

3. Mariamne Johnes, Thomas's daughter, suffered a life of poor health and died young. Her relief from illness was gardening and she became a good botanist, enjoying a long correspondence with leading botanists of the day. Her own garden, designed by one such botanist, is now being restored. Restoration work has already revealed that several rare species still flourished in the thick undergrowth. The centrepiece of Mariamne's Garden was an urn of Carrera marble sculpted by Thomas Banks. The relief carving on the urn – which is now in the National Library of Wales, Aberystwyth – showed Mariamne mourning the death of a pet robin.

The walk also passes through what was the Flower Garden of Jane Johnes, Thomas's wife, which is also being restored. Mrs Johnes's garden was planted with rhododendron, camellias and magnolia, amongst other shrubs, but was named for the wealth of wildflowers, particularly alpines.

4. The Bedford Monument is named for Francis, the 5th Duke of Bedford, a friend of Thomas Johnes and one who shared his interest in horticulture. It was designed by William Fuller Pocock and erected in 1805.

WALK 5C

NORTH

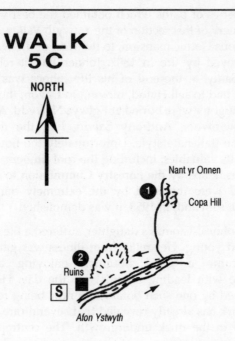

Nant yr Onnen

Copa Hill

Ruins

S

Afon Ystwyth

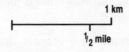

1 km

½ mile

Walk Directions   [-] denotes Point of Interest

1. From the car park [1] follow the track west towards Pendre, but soon bear left on a path which follows the edge of Cefn Creigiau, to the left. Soon a fine old beech tree is seen off to the right. Beyond it is Middle Hill, on the lower, western, slope of which was Thomas Johnes's Hafod mansion [2].

2. Beyond the beech tree the path rises to reach Mariamne's Garden [3] and just beyond, at the bottom of the steps, the Bedford Monument[4].

3. From the monument, walk down a zig-zag path which was once the carriage drive from the Hafod mansion. Go over a bridge and continue to where a sign points out a sharp left turn. Here the walk leaves the carriage drive in favour of an old walk beside Afon Ystwyth. Follow the path to a beautifully sited picnic area.

4. Just beyond the picnic site there is a footbridge on the right. Do not cross this: instead, bear left, following a path through Mrs. Johnes's Flower Garden [3]. The path now climbs gently, bearing right below the Bedford Monument and crossing the eastern flank of Cefn Creigiau to return to the start.

Walk 5c
Points of Interest:

1. The Cwmystwyth mines produced lead and copper, the copper being found chiefly on Copper Hill, or Copa Hill, which is drained on its western side by Nant yr Onnen.

The hill's copper ore was exposed by *hushing*, a process in which artificial reservoirs were created on the hillside by building dams and diverting streams. The dams were then broken, the rush of water down the hillside scouring away the soil and revealing the ore. The hushing scars which radiate out from Nant yr Onnen are believed to be the finest remains of this destructive technique in Britain.

2. In 1872 the Cwmystwyth Mine was noted as being 'both the richest and the oldest wrought mine in the county (of Ceredigion) having produced considerably more than two million sterling of lead ore'. That money came from the extraction and crushing of perhaps 100,000 tons of rock. In the early days of the mine the shafts were dug horizontally (they were called adits rather than shafts and actually sloped slightly so that water would drain naturally from them). Only when a method of powering pumps was discovered could vertical shafts be sunk. At Cwmystwyth the power source was a 30ft water-wheel.

Vertical digging had the advantage of making it easier to reach the lodes, but made extracting the ore more difficult. In a horizontal adit the ore could be loaded on to carriages which could be wheeled out on fixed tracks. Vertical shafts meant that the ore had to be hauled upwards. At first this was done by hand-driven winches. Later horses were used, then the winding frames that are such a familiar feature of coal mines. The ore was lifted out in a kibble, basically a very large bucket which could be inverted so as to unload the ore.

By the last years of the 19th century the mine was finding it hard to compete and it finally closed in 1921.

Walk Directions   [-] denotes Point of Interest

1. From the road, go down to the river and turn left (eastwards), following Afon Ystwyth upstream to the far end of the mine site. Through the steep gash in the rocks at Grid Reference 809 750 flows Nant yr Onnen [1].

2. Nant yr Onnen forces the walker up on to the road. Turn left here for a closer view of the mine building ruins [2]. But please be cautious – the ruins, though tempting, are unstable and could be dangerous.

Refreshments

There are picnic sites at The Arch and Hafod, and none of the walks are far from Pontarfynach where there are several possibilities.

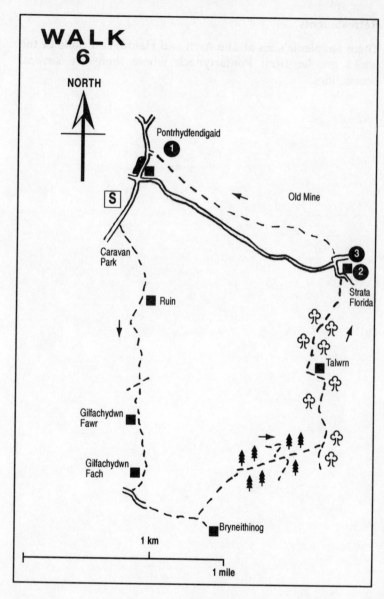

WALK 6

NORTH

Pontrhydfendigaid **1**

Old Mine

S

Caravan Park

■ Ruin

■ Gilfachydwn Fawr

■ Gilfachydwn Fach

■ Bryneithinog

3
■ **2**
Strata Florida

■ Talwrn

1 km

1 mile

Ystrad Fflur (Strata Florida)

OS Maps:	Landranger Sheet 147 (Elan Valley and Builth Wells)
	Explorer Sheet 187 (Llandovery/Llanymddyfri)
Start:	Pontrhydfendigaid
Access:	Pontrhydfendigaid lies at the junction of the B4343 which links Tregaron to Pontarfynach and the B4340 which heads north-westwards to Aberystwyth. Pontrhydfendigaid is the terminus of ArrivaCymru bus 561 from Aberystwyth.
Parking:	Parking is available, with care, in the village, but is easier in a large layby beside the B4343 to the south of the village, and on the route. There is also good parking at the Ystrad Fflur abbey site but this is strictly reserved for visitors to the ruins.
Grade:	Difficult. The walk is long and poorly way-marked and care must be taken with route findings. The walk directions reflect this, being very exact: please study them carefully.

Points of Interest:

1. The village is named for the *pont* (bridge) built across Afon Teifi so that those approaching Ystrad Fflur/Strata Florida would not have to use the *rhyd fendigaid* (the blessed ford). It is a straggling, but likeable, place with a good cafe and inn.

2. Strata Florida is the Latin form of the Welsh Ystrad Fflur, the valley of Afon Fflur that also runs into Cors Caron, parallel to, but 2 miles (3.5 kilometres) south of, Afon Teifi. The reason is that the abbey was originally sited 2 miles (3.5 kilometres) to the

south-west in a field that is still called Yr Hen Fynachlog (the old monastery). The founding of the abbey is generally ascribed to Robert FitzStephen who held large tracts of West Wales, and the agreed date is around 1160, some 100 years after the Conquest. The benefaction, so far into Wales, was fraught with danger: within two years Rhys ap Gruffudd had attacked the local Norman strongholds and taken FitzStephen prisoner.

The abbey that FitzStephen had founded was Cistercian, an order which extolled the virtues of simplicity, hard work in agriculture, and extreme poverty. It seems that the quiet dignity of the house won Rhys over, a charter of 1184 naming him as the builder of the abbey. Though some work may have been carried out during his rule of Ceredigion, the building of Ystrad Fflur occupied a very long period, the Chapter House having been completed only in 1235, and the bell only being bought in 1254. The cost of the bell was 97 marks and two cows.

Despite its Norman foundations the abbey became, perhaps because of its remoteness from England, a great centre for Welsh culture and an influential voice in Welsh politics. When Llywelyn Fawr (Llywelyn the Great) of Gwynedd decided to assemble Welsh lords and princes together so as to swear their allegiance to his son Dafydd, it was to Ystrad Fflur that he called them in 1238. It is said that within the cemetery many of these princes, and also princes from later ages, are buried. The abbey has, for this reason, been called the Welsh Westminster. It fared badly during the time of Owain Glyndŵr. In 1401 the army of Henry IV was being harried by Glyndŵr's guerrilla fighters and a baggage train belonging to his young son, Henry, was also attacked and robbed. King Henry was furious and marched on Ystrad Fflur determined to vent his anger on this symbol of Welshness. The abbey was plundered, its holy vessels stolen, its buildings looted, and many monks were murdered. Henry ordered that his knights' horses should be tethered at the high altar, with inevitable consequences for the church. His knights drank the abbey's wine cellars dry in a two-day drunken spree, then smashed down the buildings and fired the ruins. In later life Henry is said to have been in an agony of conscience over the acts, though this must have been much later as his son quartered an army here in 1407 during the siege of Aberystwyth castle.

The holiness of the spot meant that, when peace returned, the abbey was rebuilt, and was in constant occupation up until the time of its dissolution. Despite the ravages suffered by the abbey in the early 15th century and an earlier fire following a lightning strike, there is a considerable amount of Norman work in the abbey, including a superb Norman doorway. Not much else of the structure remains intact. Following dissolution the abbeys were customarily stripped of the lead from their roofs and over a period of time the walls collapsed, a decay assisted by locals who used the buildings as a convenient quarry. As a consequence little remains that is immediately discernible to the layman. Nevertheless the site still has a quiet dignity.

3. As a contrast to the abbey's cemetery, resting place of many of the medieval princes of Wales, the cemetery of the church beside it holds the remains of Dafydd ap Gwilym one of the greatest medieval poets of Europe. Traditionally Dafydd (who died in the late 14th century) was buried under the yew tree, though the memorials to him are very recent. Dafydd was born at Penrhyncoch near Aberystwyth and is renowned for his prose poems on all subjects from love to humour. He is especially fine at describing the natural world.

Walk Directions   [-] denotes Point of Interest

1. From the lay-by at the southern edge of Pontrhydfendigaid [1], continue south along the road towards Tregaron, going gently uphill and soon reaching a stile and an ancient wooden footpath sign on the left.

2. Cross the stile and follow the green track beyond towards the caravans. Go on to the caravan site road and bear left,

between the vans. As the road bears right, bear left past the last caravan to reach a stile in the corner.

3. Cross and follow the fence on the left, going through a gate to reach a ruin, off to the left. There, bear right, going through a gate opening and maintaining direction uphill to reach a stile in the fence at the top of the field. The stile is to the right of the woodland edge beyond. Cross and follow the fence on the left to another stile. Cross and go diagonally right across a field to reach a gate in the top right corner. Go through and turn left immediately through another gate. Now go diagonally right towards a barn.

4. Go through the gate beside the barn and along the farm lane opposite. Beyond the first farm (Gilfachydwn Fawr) the lane degenerates to a tractor track, but remains obvious. Go through a gate and follow the now rugged track uphill to a second farm (Gilfachydwn Fach). Go through a gate here and straight ahead along the farm lane to reach a road. There is a fine view from here of the high moorland of the mid-Wales plateau.

5. Turn left. When the road ends, go through a gate and follow the farm lane beyond. As you approach the farm, a second lane comes in from the left: take this, following it uphill. As it approaches a barn, go through a gate on the left and turn right along the fence (negotiating a curious piece of fencing) to reach a gate into the forest.

6. Follow the clear bridleway through the forest to reach a forestry road. Maintain direction along this for 50 metres but, as it goes sharp right, bear left along another bridleway between the trees. Follow the bridleway through increasingly excellent woodland to reach a crossing track. Bear left – there is a waymarker here (a blue arrow on a white circle, the waymarker for the unofficial Cambrian Way long-distance footpath – see Walk 7).

7. Follow the track to a gate and continue along the green lane

beyond to reach a ruin (Talwrn). Go left along the ruin's near wall to reach another green lane, following it to its end. Go through a gate and turn right, following a stream. Soon, bear left to reach a gate, bearing right beyond it to regain the stream.

8. A not always obvious path now follows the stream downhill, crossing it once, to reach a footbridge. Cross and follow the stream bank to a gate. Turn left along the road beyond. The Strata Florida car park is to the left, the ruins [2] and church [3] to the right.

9. As the road turns sharp left, go right past the telephone box and, soon, go over a waymarked stile on the left. Cross a footbridge and a waymarked stile by a gate. The path now follows Afon Teifi – to your left – all the way back to Pontrhydfendigaid, with occasional waymarker posts to point the way and a series of stiles and gates to cross. The bank of the river has some lovely trees, mainly hazel and oak. During the early section of this part of the walk, the ruins of an old lead mine can be seen off to the right.

10. When you reach a farm lane, bear left along it to reach the village road. Turn left, crossing the humpbacked bridge over Afon Teifi and passing the road, on the left, for Ystrad Fflur (Strata Florida), to return to the start.

Refreshments

There are an inn and a cafe in Pontrhydfendigaid.

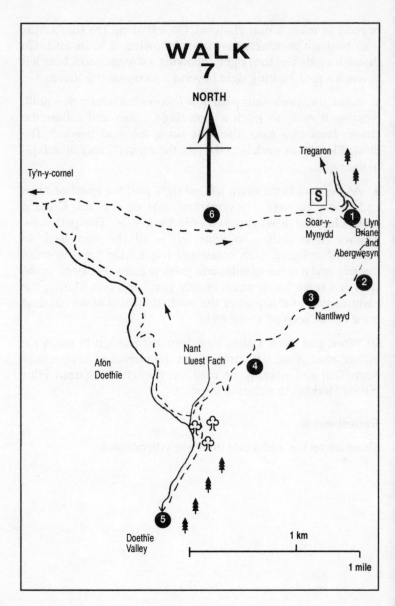

WALK

7

NORTH

Tregaron

Ty'n-y-cornel

S Soar-y-
Mynydd

1 Llyn
Brianne
and
Abergwesyn

2

3 Nantllwyd

6

Afon
Doethïe

Nant
Lluest Fach

4

5

Doethïe
Valley

1 km

1 mile

6 miles (10 kilometres)
or 10 miles (16 kilometres)

Deepest Elenydd

OS Maps:	Landranger Sheet 146 (Lampeter and Llandovery) Explorer Sheet 187 (Llandovery/Llanymddyfri)
Start:	Soar-y-mynydd Chapel, at Grid Reference 784 533
Access:	The chapel lies beside a minor road which reaches the north tip of Llyn Brianne where it forks for Abergwesyn (to the east) and Rhandir-mwyn (to the south). To the north-west this minor road crosses remote country to reach Tregaron. There is no public transport to this chapel.
Parking:	There is ample parking at the chapel
Grade:	Difficult. Though the paths are reasonable, this is rugged, remote country

Points of Interest:

1. Farming on the mid-Wales plateau, the land of Elenydd, has always been a lonely occupation. In 1740 the Rev. Howell Harris held a service in Rhiwalog Farm, near Soar-y-mynydd, the local farmers and their families riding to it on horseback. The services were popular, not only because they allowed the farming families to worship their God in their own language, but because they were a social occasion, a chance to meet and talk with neighbours. After Harris's death the tradition was maintained, the preachers including William Williams Pantycelyn, the famous Llandymddyfri-born hymn writer. The tradition lasted 80 years. Then, in 1822, the Rev. Ebenezer Richard vicar of Tregaron and father of Henry Richard, the

Apostle of Peace (see Walk 8), built Soar-y-mynydd chapel on land donated by John Jones of Nantllwyd Farm. It is still claimed to be the most remote chapel in Wales. After its construction it was the custom for local farmers to offer hospitality to the preachers, fetching them on horseback from Tregaron or Llanddewi Brefi on Saturday and giving them a meal, bed and breakfast. By 1960 congregations had dropped to just 10, but the chapel then saw something of a revival. It is now considered an honour to take the service and congregations have doubled. On the last Sunday in August, a special service often attracts over 50 car-loads of visitors. Inside the chapel the oak chair in the pulpit is a memorial to John Hughes Williams, murdered in 1983, who was instrumental in keeping Soar open when congregations dwindled in the 1960s.

2. This walk follows a section of the Cambrian Way, a proposed long-distance footpath across the mountainous backbone of Wales, linking Cardiff and Conwy. The Way was to have been an official National Trail, but the Countryside Commission, which had the task of creating the route, was unable to tread the tortuous path between the various pro- and anti- factions and, eventually, the idea was abandoned. Drawing on the research of the Commission's field officers the author of this guide has produced another to an 'unofficial' Cambrian Way, which uses rights of way to link Cardiff and Conwy, maintaining the spirit (and almost the exact line) of the proposed route. See *The Cambrian Way* by Richard Sale, published by Gwasg Carreg Gwalch.

3. Around Nantllwyd there was once a thriving community, the remains of over 25 squatters' farms having been discovered. Such farms were built to take advantage of a 15th century law that gave a man the right to a parcel of land if, starting at dusk, he could raise four walls and a chimney and have a fire burning by the dawn of the next day.

4. The walk crosses a section of the high mid-Wales plateau, an

area which Giraldus Cambrensis (Gerald of Wales) called Elenydd. Gerald was Archdeacon of Brecon in the late 12th century and undertook his famous journey as companion to Baldwin, Archbishop of Canterbury, who was seeking support, in 1188, for the Third Crusade. Gerald used the name to describe the whole of the mountain area of south Wales, as opposed to Eryri, the mountains of north Wales. However, since Giraldus recognised the individual mountain blocks of the Cambrian Mountains what he probably meant by Elenydd was that area between Pumlumon and Mynydd Du. It is likely that the name derives from Afon Elan to the north of the area.

5. The Doethïe valley is one of the finest in mid-Wales, a tight rugged valley, its sides studded with rocky outcrops and wind-bent trees. Near the point where Afon Doethïe joins Afon Tywi the country is a haven for wildlife, there being an RSPB reserve (Dinas) and a National Nature Reserve. The local area played a crucial role in re-establishing the red kite. Once the red kite was common all over Britain, even being recorded in medieval London scavenging among the rubbish that was the norm in conurbations of that time. But better hygiene in cities and gamekeepers in the country (who saw the birds as a threat to young grouse and pheasants) led to a catastrophic decline in numbers. By the end of the 19th century the red kite had been made extinct in England and Scotland and was also declining in Wales. By the 1960s a mere handful of pairs (perhaps as few as six) clung on in the wilderness of mid-Wales. The kite is largely a carrion feeder, though it will take live rabbits and rodents. It takes young birds, too, but these are more likely to be gulls or crows: the red kite was never the threat to game birds that the gamekeepers feared. It also needs trees in which to perch and nest. The country near the Doethïe valley was ideal and it was here that the main effort was made to halt the decline in numbers and then to promote an increase. This has been remarkably successful. By 1989 the RSPB/Nature Conservation Council were able to release red kites into England – they used

birds from Spain and Sweden rather than Wales, but the Welsh population was by then showing a healthy population rise. Birds have now also been released in Scotland. In 1998 there were over 150 breeding pairs of kites in Wales, as well as about 75 pairs in England and 20 in Scotland.

The red kite is a magnificent bird, a rich chestnut-brown in colour and with a deeply forked tail. Walkers in the Doethïe valley are very likely to see one: its appearance, working the updrafts from the steep valley sides, is likely to be the highlight of the day.

6. This track is part of an old drovers' road from Llanddewibrefi, continuing eastwards beyond Soar chapel towards the border with England. In the days before refrigeration, cattle, pigs and sheep, and even chickens, turkeys and geese, were brought to market live, drovers escorting the animals along defined drove-roads. A big drove must have been a magnificent sight and the drovers certainly earned their pay – imagine having to keep flocks of fowls on the move as well as the herds. It is said that the birds had their feet dipped in pitch to harden them for the march and that cattle were shod to ease the load on their feet. The blacksmiths who shoed the cattle were said to be both highly skilled and extremely brave, both of which seem to be indisputable.

Inns were set up along the roads for the use of the drovers, who were rich on their return journeys and, therefore, very popular with landlords. The rich drovers were also popular with highwaymen who lay in wait on quieter sections of the roads. It was to try to combat the highwaymen and to reduce the losses of heavy drinking that banks such as Tregaron's Black Sheep Bank (see Walk 8) were established.

One famous drover was Twm Siôn Cati. He was the illegitimate son of Catherine Jones of Tregaron, who named him Thomas Jones. Because of his lack of a legitimate father, he became known as Twm Siôn Cati. He was a man of some renown, and referred to by poets, during his own lifetime. Born about 1530, he married a Brecon widow late in life and was a justice of peace for the old shires of Brecon and Carmarthen and Major of Brecon. His will, dated 17 May 1609, still exists – he left nine head of cattle to an illegitimate son and everything else to his widow Johan (Joan) – but the legends surrounding him, which transform him into a Welsh Robin Hood type of figure, but one with rather more humour and a great deal less tragedy than the original, are largely the work of Llewelyn Pritchard, an early 19th century writer. One story of Twm, related by a local to George Borrow and recounted in his book *Wild Wales*, tells of Twm stealing a bull with a short tail and attaching a longer tail to the short one before taking it to market to sell. There the original owner recognises the bull, but is surprised by the long tail. He claims the tail must be false, so Twm takes a knife and cuts it off, taking care to cut the real tail above the false one. The bull roars, blood flows and the farmer, convinced he has made a mistake, apologises to Twm. But Twm now insists the farmer buy the bull, claiming he only mutilated it at his request. The people who had gathered to watch the incident side with Twm and the farmer is forced to buy his own stolen bull at a high price.

Twm's reputed hideout during his 'loveable rogue' period was on the RSPB's Dinas reserve, at Grid Reference 786466.

Walk Directions   [-] denotes Point of Interest

1. From the chapel [1] follow the obvious path [2] heading south-eastwards (over the cattle grid, along the track signed 'Locked Gate Ahead') bearing right when this forks. The track now continues straightforwardly to Nantllwyd Farm [3].

2. Negotiate the farm by going between the buildings and through the gates, continuing along the clear moorland path [4], climbing gently and crossing a couple of streams which drain the plateau. Beyond the second stream the path crosses a broad ridge, then descends steeply to reach a path fork close to the

Nant Lluest Fach.

3. The right-hand path here is the return route. For the moment, bear left and follow the clear path through woodland to reach Afon Doethïe. Now follow the river southwards [5]. This is an out – and – back detour and can be of any length: to savour this magnificent valley it should be walked at least as far as Craig Cnwch-glas (on the valley's eastern side, at Grid Reference 766 494).

4. After the detour along the Doethïe valley, return to the path fork near Nant Lluest Fach and take the other branch. This also drops to Afon Doethïe, but follows the river northwards through exquisite country to reach, after about 3.5 kilometres – just over 2 miles – a crossing track. To the left the track goes to the remote Youth Hostel of Ty'n-y-cornel. To the right it can be followed [6] all the way to Capel Soar. The chapel can be reached from the track end by way of a charming rustic bridge.

Refreshments

None. Walkers must bring their own or drive to Tregaron (the closest) Rhandir-mwyn or Abergwesyn.

Tregaron

OS Maps:	Landranger Sheet 146 (Lampeter and Llandovery) Explorer Sheets 199 (Lampeter/Llanbedr Pont Steffan) and 187 (Llandovery/Llanymddyfri)
Start:	The statue of Henry Richard in the centre of Tregaron.
Access:	Tregaron lies on Afon Brennig where the A485 Lampeter to Aberystwyth road crosses the B4343 (Lampeter to Pontrhydfendigaid road). The town is served by ArrivaCymru buses from Aberystwyth, and the Brodyr James buses that link Lampeter and Pontrhydfendigaid.
Parking:	Available with care in the town. There is limited car parking in the main square.
Grade:	Moderate. The walk is on good paths or minor roads throughout, but involves some 400ft (130m) of climbing.

Points of Interest:

1. Henry Richard was born in Tregaron in 1812 and became a minister in the Congregational Church. He served as minister in the Marlborough Church in London from 1835 to 1850. In 1848, while still a minister in London, he was appointed secretary of the Peace Society in which he had been a leading light for many years. He was the editor of the Society's monthly magazine *Herald of Peace* and a close friend of its leading activists John Bright and Richard Cobden. As secretary of the Society he attended peace conferences in Europe. These conferences are often seen as the forerunners of the League of Nations/United Nations. In 1868 he became MP for Merthyr Tudful and became

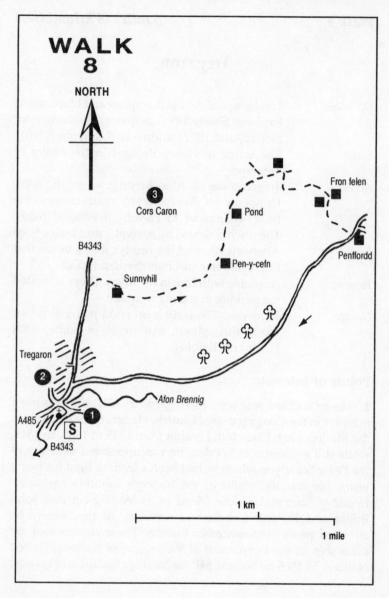

WALK 8

NORTH

③ Cors Caron

Fron felen

Pond

B4343

Pen-y-cefn

Penffordd

Sunnyhill

Tregaron

Afon Brennig

②

A485

① S

B4343

1 km

1 mile

known at Westminster as the Member of Wales for his campaigning on behalf of not only his constituents but all Welshmen. He felt that the English-dominated parliament did not understand the Welsh way of life and attempted to rectify that situation. Henry Richard was known towards the end of his life as the 'Apostle of Peace' and died in 1888. The bronze statue of him was erected by the proud townsfolk in 1893.

2. Tregaron is the town of Caron, an early Celtic saint reputedly buried beneath the mound on which St Caron's Church now stands, though in reality the mound is likely to cover a pre-historic burial.

George Barrow visited Tregaron during his 19th century walk through Wales which he related in *Wild Wales*. On approaching the village he was 'put very much in mind of an Andalusian village overhung by its sierra'. Barrow was clearly a man of imagination for Tregaron is a typical Welsh market town, almost impossible to mistake for anything else. At the time of the drovers (see Walk 7) it was one of the most important towns in mid-Wales and home of Banc y Ddafad Ddu (Bank of the Black Sheep), into which the more sensible drovers paid the cash they had received for their work. The number of sheep on the banknotes indicated the note's value. During the Napoleonic wars the bank collapsed causing considerable local hardship.

In addition to the prosperity brought by the drovers, the town also had a thriving wool industry with cloth factories and cottage-based knitters and tailors. The coming of the railways ended the droving (though it did bring its own prosperity), and when the wool industry also declined sharply many townsfolk moved to the valleys of South Wales. The local fairs and markets remained and these allowed Tregaron to remain an important local town.

Our walk starts close to the Talbot Hotel where George Barrow enjoyed 'an excellent supper and a very comfortable night', full justification for his having been told that it was a 'very good inn . . . where they are always glad to see English gentlemen'. Across the square from the Talbot is the town church. The oldest section dates from medieval times and once housed the town school. In the newer section there is a superb ironwork screen, the gift of a local family in the early 20th century in memory of their young son, killed when a small herd of horses were frightened into stampede. A recent ex-vicar was local-born George Noakes, the present Bishop of St David's.

3. Cors Caron formed when moraine deposited by the Ice Age glacier, which widened the Teifi valley, blocked the valley. Behind the moraine dam a shallow lake formed. This filled with sediment and, as water levels fell, formed the bog. To decay completely, dead plant life needs oxygen and bacteria. Waterlogged soil prevents oxygen reaching the dead matter, and the slightly acid water of the Teifi valley inhibits bacteria. The plant matter does not therefore decay completely, forming a jelly-like mass – peat. The peat bog supports sphagnum moss and a collection of interesting plants – purple moorgrass, cottongrasses and rarer varieties such as the insectivorous sundew. Birds include the red kite and hen harrier, animals include otters, water voles and polecats. Cors Caron is one of the largest and most important bogs surviving in Britain and access to it is controlled. Visitors can follow the old railway line from the B4343 north of Tregaron to the old Ystrad Fflur station on the B4340 – there is an observation tower (at Grid Reference 705 647) along the way – but to follow the footpath through the inner bog a permit is required (contact the Countryside Council for Wales, Neuaddlas, Tregaron, Tel: 01974 298480).

The south-eastern edge of the bog is traced by the line of the old Aberystwyth to Caerfyrddin (Carmarthen) railway line. There was insufficient solid ground at the foot of the ridge taken by the walk on which to lay a line and so it was laid across the bog, the lines carried on bales of wool and wooden faggots. The line lasted for exactly one hundred years, opening in 1866 and closing in 1966.

Walk Directions   [-] denotes Point of Interest

1. From the statue of Henry Richard [1], walk away from the Talbot Hotel passing the church on your left. Cross Afon Brennig and turn right to follow the B4343 north (towards Pontrhydfendigaid), walking through the northern section of Tregaron. [2]

2. Follow the road for a little over 1/2 mile (1 kilometre) to reach a house on the left. Just beyond, take the road on the right to Sunnyhill. The road is unmarked: look for the tree stump in the triangle at the junction. Follow the road past Sunnyhill Farm, on the right, and continue along it – it becomes a bridleway – with a fine view to the left across Cors Caron (Tregaron Bog) [3].

3. Follow the track uphill past Pen-y-cefn Farm and continue to reach a small pond on the right. Here a path continues ahead. Do not take this: instead, continue along the track which bears right, then descends to reach a junction of tracks.

4. Maintain direction, soon reaching a farmhouse on the left. Now ignore the gate/track ahead, turning right through another gate and following the track beyond to reach yet another gate. Do not go through this: instead, turn left and walk beside the hedge (on your left), soon passing the ruins of an old building on the right.

5. Contour around the ridge end on a clear path/track, with boggy land down on the left, going through several gates to reach Fronfelen Farm.

6. Go past the farmhouse (to your right), following a track downhill to reach a minor road near Penffordd. Turn right and follow the road – though narrow it is very quiet – to reach the B4343 on the northern outskirts of Tregaron.

7. Turn left to retrace the early section of the walk to return to the statue.

Refreshments

There is plenty of choice in Tregaron.

Llanddewibrefi

OS Maps:	Landranger Sheet 146 (Lampeter and Llandovery) Explorer Sheet 199 (Lampeter/Llanbedr Pont Steffan)
Start:	The church of Llanddewibrefi.
Access:	The village of Llanddewibrefi lies on the B4343 a few miles south of Tregaron. The village is on the route of Brodyr James buses 588 and 589 from Lampeter to Pontrhydfendigaid.
Parking:	Available with care in the village.
Grade:	Easy. A delightful short walk on good paths/ tracks and quiet lanes.

Points of Interest:

1. The earliest parts of the church dates from the 12th century, but the main body was substantially rebuilt in the early 19th century after it had partially collapsed. Within the church are a series of five incised stones dating from the 7th – 9th centuries making them some of the oldest in Wales. Four of these have Latin crosses, one an additional inscription *Cenlisini BT DS*, meaning 'the cross of Cenlisinus, may God bless him'. Another is inscribed *Dallvs Dvmelvs* (Dallus Dumelus, an Irish/Celtic name). All the stones are gravestones. A sixth stone, easily the most historically important, was broken up in 1812 and used as building stone for the church. Its inscription had been transcribed by Edward Lluyd in 1699 and read *Hic Iacet Idnert Filivs Iacobi Qvi Occisvs Fvit Propter Predom Sancti David* meaning 'Here lies Idnert, son of Jacob, who was killed because of the plunder of Saint David' and presumably refers to a defence of an early church against a bandit raid. The stone is dated to the 7th

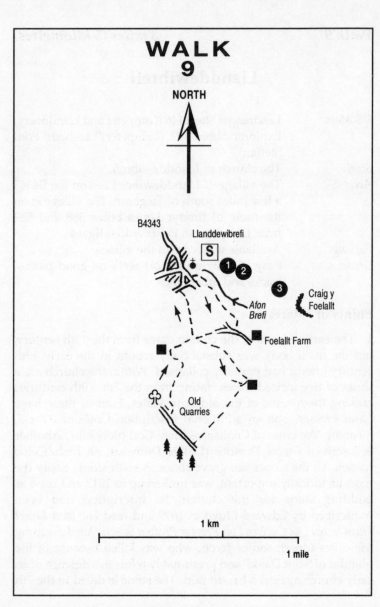

WALK
9

NORTH

B4343

Llanddewibrefi

S

1 2

3

Craig y
Foelallt

Afon Brefi

Foelallt Farm

Old Quarries

1 km

1 mile

century and is the earliest reference to the patron saint of Wales, having been inscribed less than a century after his death in 589. One section of this stone can be seen on the outside of the west wall of the nave, in the north-west corner.

2. In the late 4th century a Celtic monk – probably born in the north of Ireland and called Morgan (which means 'from the sea') because of this – began to preach a form of Christianity that was at odds with that of the established church. He denied the inevitability of original sin, emphasising the importance of an individual's willpower in living a Christian life, and claiming that this was as important as divine grace in ensuring the salvation of the soul. Morgan also seems to have had a leaning towards reincarnation, his philosophy having much in common with Buddhism, though he was opposed to any idea of predestination. In Rome the troublesome monk was known under his Greek/Latin name of Pelagius – a translation of 'from the sea'.

Christianity was by now the state religion of the Roman Empire and the ideas of Pelagius were a threat to the new-found power of the church which was promoting the idea of salvation through divine grace alone, an idea which enhanced its power. Pelagius' ideas were specifically opposed by St Augustine of Hippo and were declared to be heretical by the Synod of Carthage in 418. In Wales, however, what became known as the Pelagian heresy had great popular appeal. In broadest terms, the Welsh believed that 'I should do, therefore I ought to' which represented a threat to the central position of the church in the community. Consequently, in the early 6th century a synod was organised at which the opposing philosophies could be discussed and a decision made. The place chosen for the synod was Llanddewibrefi, now a tiny, though picturesque, village and not the place where you might expect such a momentous event to take place. It is conjectured that the site, on Afon Brefi, but close to Afon Teifi, was already an important religious centre. The earliest form of religious site in Wales was the *llan*, a place where a holy man or teacher would construct a small earthwork or wooden church where he could live a life of abstinence and piety while instructing the locals. Sometimes a religious community, a *clas*, would develop around the *llan*. Possibly there was such a clas at Llanddewibrefi.

St David had decided not to attend the synod, but so many arrived and tried to speak that the meeting soon became chaotic. Reluctantly St David agreed to come to restore order. He addressed the crowd and as he did a mound miraculously rose beneath his feet lifting him into the air so that everyone could see him. A white dove also landed on his shoulder. This is represented in a fine, life-size statue within the church. St David spoke against the Pelagian heresy and his great speech carried the day – though it was not until the Council of Whitby in 664 that the Roman Church achieved a final victory over the Celtic Church.

The importance of the synod, and the miracles associated with St David, made Llanddewibrefi an important place and a college was set up, flourishing until the early medieval period. *Llyfr Ancr Llanddewibrefi* (The Book of the Anchorite), one of the most important items in the Bodley Library, Oxford, was written at Llanddewibrefi's college in 1346. The book quotes St David's last message to his followers.

3. The village's curious name derives from a synod attended by St David (Dewi Sant) – see Point 2 above – and from an ancient legend that it was founded by Huw Gadarn (Huw the Mighty), who led the original Celts to Britain from central Europe. Huw's standard was emblazoned with an ox as he had bred a huge form of long-horned oxen called *Ychen Bannog*. Huw is said to have built the first church at Llanddewi – though as he is said to have arrived in Wales over a thousand years before the birth of Christ this story necessitates a belief in pre-Christian Christianity – starting it with a vast stone which his *ychen bannog* dragged from the hills to the north-east. The dragged stone created a furrow (a *cwys*) in the ground. This is still called

Cwys-yr-Ychen Bannog and can be seen on the hills of Y Bryn and Garn Gron to the north-east of Tregaron. The true nature of this curious feature is not known.

Sadly the effort of dragging the stone was too great for one ox: when the stone lodged against a rock the hauling caused its heart to fail. The second ox, heartbroken by the loss of its companion, bellowed nine times then itself died. Ironically the bellowing split the offending rock. The bellow *(brefi)* named Afon Brefi which in turn named the village, to distinguish it from all the other Llanddewis. The rock that was split by the bellowing, Craig y Foelallt, is seen from the route.

A horn that was said to have been from one of these mighty oxen – called *Corn yr Ych* – was once kept in the church. Its base was a huge 17 inches (43 cms) in diameter. Sadly it was broken, but a fragment can still be seen in the Welsh Folk Museum at St Fagans.

Walk Directions   [-] denotes Point of Interest

1. From the church [1], [2], go back to the road and turn left, through the southern end of the village [3].

2. Soon, fork left, and then turn left along the 'No Through Road'. Now bear right along a signed track, following it past some cottages, to the right, and into a field. Walk along the edge of the field (fence to the right) to reach a kissing gate. Go through, cross a ditch and turn right along the edge of the field beyond. Bear right in the corner to reach a stile on the left, by a gate.

3. Cross the stile on to a minor road. To the left from here is Foelallt Farm. Across Afon Brefi from the farm, Craig y Foelallt [3] can be seen on the hillside.

4. Turn right along the road, then bear left at a fork to reach a cross-roads of lanes/tracks. (This junction is reached again later in the walk.) Turn sharply left here along a lane past some

cottages. Bear right, passing a house (to the right) and continue along a green lane which climbs steadily – with a good view of Craig y Foelallt – to reach a farmhouse.

5. Turn sharp right then, soon, bear left along a track and continue climbing, ignoring a track on the right. Follow the track to reach a minor road opposite a forestry plantation.

6. Turn right and follow the road gently downhill. The plantation on the left ends: continue to reach a clump of trees on the right. A few yards beyond this, turn right along a track which climbs to a track junction near disused quarries on the right.

7. Turn left and follow a fenced track past more old quarries, descending gently, then more steeply to reach a farmhouse on the left.

8. Just beyond the farmhouse, turn right and descend a narrow path, soon bearing right along a walled path which is followed to the junction of tracks reached earlier in the walk from the opposite direction.

9. Now bear left to follow the track heading north towards the village. Continue along a path through several gates – going through fields, then along an enclosed path – with the church tower as a clear waymarker ahead. Beyond a kissing gate, a sports field is reached: continue along a lane, then turn right and then left on village roads to return to the start.

Refreshments

The New Inn is close to the church, and there is plenty of choice in nearby Tregaron.

Llanbedr Pont Steffan (Lampeter)

OS Maps:	Landranger Sheet 146 (Lampeter and Llandovery) Explorer Sheet 199 (Lampeter/Llanbedr Pont Steffan)
Start:	St Peter's Church, Llanbedr Pont Steffan
Access:	Llanbedr Pont Steffan lies at the junction of the A485, A482 and A475 main roads. It is served by many buses.
Parking:	There is a signed car park in the southern part of the town, towards the Secondary school and swimming pool.
Grade:	Difficult. Straightforward walking, but a long route.

Points of Interest:

1. There was a church dedicated to St Peter as early as the 13th century but, though it is thought likely that there was one during earlier times, there is no conclusive evidence. Gerald of Wales does not mention one during his visit in 1188, but a death in the church is mentioned in 1227. The medieval building was demolished in 1820 when it became ruinous. The replacement was so ugly that the townsfolk demanded its demolition, though not until 1870 was the present building completed. One interesting aspect of this final rebuild was that the new church was moved uphill a little, resulting in the tombs of medieval gentry – which had, of course, been in the chancel – being left exposed in the new churchyard.

2. Though there is evidence of human habitation from the Bronze Age, the Iron Age and the Roman period, no clear

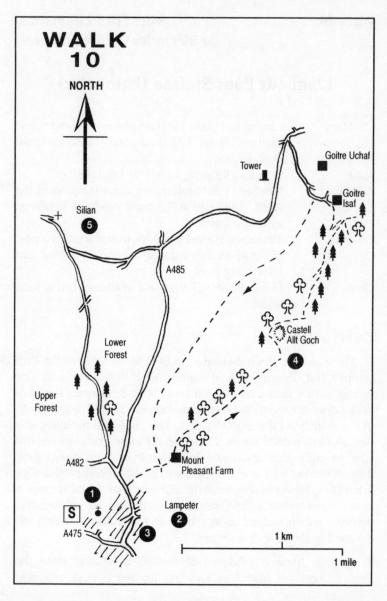

WALK 10

NORTH

Silian **5**

Tower

Goitre Uchaf

Goitre Isaf

A485

Lower Forest

Upper Forest

Castell Allt Goch **4**

A482

Mount Pleasant Farm

1

Lampeter **2**

S

A475

3

1 km

1 mile

84

evidence of a settlement survives here from before the Norman period. Shortly after the conquest, Ceredigion was occupied (in the 1190s) and motte and bailey castles were raised near this strategically important site close to where Afon Dulas runs into Afon Teifi. One *motte* (mound – the earliest Norman castles were wooden keeps on top of man-made mounds, surrounded by a wooden stockade enclosing the *bailey*, the area at the foot of the mound) can be seen in the grounds of the college. Another, Castell Bugad, stands to the east of the town near Afon Teifi. It is thought that the name of the latter comes from Sir Hugh Buged, Earl of Norfolk, who was active in Wales during the reign of King Stephen.

The old Welsh name for the town was Llanbedr Talybont Ystyfyn (the church of Peter near the end of Stephen's bridge) the bridge named maybe for the man who built the first one over Afon Teifi or maybe for the Norman King who, as noted above, was on the throne when Sir Hugh Buged built his castle here. The bridge which takes the main road over Afon Teifi, to the south of the town, is still called Pont Steffan. Today the Welsh name is Llanbedr Pont Steffan, although it is more often known simply as Llanbed.

It is likely that there was a priory in the town in early medieval times, a daughter house of Strata Florida (Ystrad Fflur), but it was never a significant contributor to the prosperity of Llanbedr Pont Steffan, that being based on its success as a market town for the surrounding area. There are records of markets, as early as the 13th century, and by the 18th century there were not only weekly markets but also eight annual fairs one of which, *Ffair Dalis*, was among the most important horse fairs in Wales.

Because of the fairs the lordship of the town was a wealthy one. It eventually fell to the Lloyd family who built a mansion (Maesyfelin) close to Afon Dulas at the northern of the town centre. The Lloyd family was both rich and influential, providing the second principal of Jesus College, Oxford and several local judges and MPs. But, in the 17th century, the family was involved in an infamous murder. At the time Rhys Pritchard was vicar of Llandymddyfri. Pritchard is famous for *Canwyll y Cymru* (The Welshman's Candle), a book of religious verse, but was equally famous at the time for his ferocious piety, his sermons invariably illuminating what he saw as the iniquities of his flock. Pritchard's son Samuel was a friend of the Lloyds and a frequent visitor to their mansion. Unfortunately he was soon having an affair with one of the ladies at the mansion. Whether the lady was one of the Lloyds or a servant girl is not clear but, whoever she was, Samuel's relationship with her was the cause of bitterness with the Lloyds. One night, several of the menfolk smothered Samuel with a pillow, put his body in a sack, and carried it to the outskirts of Llanymddyfri. There, they threw the body into Afon Tywi, hoping that everyone would believe the death to be an accidental drowning. But someone told Pritchard the truth and he cursed the Lloyds, his curse translating as:

The curse of God on Maesyfelin fall
On root of every tree, on stone of every wall
Because the flower of fair Llandovery town
Was headlong cast in Tywi's flood to drown

From that time on the fortunes of the Lloyds declined. Today nothing remains of Maesyfelin.

As the fortunes of the Lloyds were falling, those of the town were rising, with Llanbedr Pont Steffan becoming an important drovers town (see Walk 8). There is still a Drovers Road off Bridge Street. The railway built to link Caerfyrddin (Carmarthen) to Aberystwyth aided the prosperity, though its closure in 1966 was not a severe blow: Llanbed has always been a market town rather than a tourist centre, even if today it portrays itself as a good centre for visiting mid-Wales.

3. It is an astonishing fact that here, in this small mid-Wales market town, sits the oldest University in England and Wales

after Oxford and Cambridge. It was founded by Thomas Burgess, Bishop of St David's, who from 1804 gathered funds to create a college for Welsh students who were financially unable to enrol at Oxford or Cambridge. The land at Llanbedr Pont Steffan – known as Castle Field because of the motte of the Norman Castle – was given to Burgess for his college by John Harford and the foundation stone was laid on 12 August 1822. St David's College was designed by Charles Cockerell who modelled it on the Oxbridge colleges, and opened to its first students on St David's Day, 1 March 1827, the college chapel being consecrated a few months later. The initial buildings, which included a library, cost £20,000, a vast sum for the time and a tribute to Bishop Burgess' enthusiasm and far-sightedness.

At first St David's was solely a theological college and, even though it was granted the right to award degrees as early as 1852, it did not become a college of the University of Wales when that was founded in 1893 (with three colleges – Bangor, Cardiff and Aberystwyth). Unfortunately, by the 1950s a falling role threatened the future of the college. It was supported by University College, Cardiff but also widened its choice of study areas. Finally, in 1971 it became St David's University College, a full college of the University of Wales, though the name will soon change, dropping 'St David's', in keeping with that of the other colleges of the University of Wales. Today the college has around 1,500 students in many disciplines. Visitors to Llanbed are welcome to stroll around the college grounds and to visit the chapel.

4. Castell Allt Goch is a typical Iron Age hill-fort, a single ditch and rampart enclosing an oval area of about 3 acres. On the eastern side of the fort, where the slope of the hill is more gentle, the defences are enhanced by two further ditches and ramparts.

5. Built into the external face of the south wall of the church, near the west end, is a stone with a Latin inscription which

reads either *Silbandvs Iacit or Fili Bandvs Iacit*, either 'Silbandus lies here' or 'the son of Bandus lies here'. The stone is dated to the 5th or early 6th century, a remarkable survival. The incised cross is later, perhaps 7th century, though it could be later still. Inside the church there is another early stone, probably dating from the 9th or 10th century and with intricate patterns incised on the two faces.

Walk Directions   [-] denotes Point of Interest

1. From the church [1], walk down to the main road (A475) and turn left through the town [2]. At the junction of the A475 and A485 – the centre of the town – turn left along College Street, the A485/A582 for Aberaeron and Tregaron.

2. Walk past the University [3], to the right, and continue along the main road, passing the University bookshop, the war memorial and the Gorsedd circle to the left.

3. Just beyond the rugby field, to the right, turn right on a road signed as a bridleway, that runs beside the field. The road becomes a rough track: continue along it, crossing a tributary stream of Afon Teifi. Just beyond, the shorter version of the walk returns on the left. Follow the track uphill to Mount Pleasant Farm.

4. At the farm bear left on a signed path at the edge of woodland. Go through a gate and follow the path beyond through superb woodland to reach two stiles.

5. Ignore the stile to the left, crossing the one ahead and walking beside the wood. Cross two stiles and continue to reach two gates. Cross the stile by the left gate and take the avenue of oaks, birch and ash to reach another stile.

6. Cross the stile and turn left (signed as a bridleway), walking with fine beech trees (and a fence) on the left. Castell Allt Goch [4] is to the right. At the bottom of the field, turn right and

follow a raised bank. To the left, the prominent 'chimney' is a folly tower on the Derry Ormond estate. Built in the 19th century, the top of the tower – from which there was an impressive view – was reached by a spiral stairway. The tower is now ruinous and cannot be climbed so the quality of the view cannot now be verified.

7. Ignore a yellow arrow pointing left, following the blue arrow ahead but, where the bank swings sharp right, cross a stile on the left and follow a narrow path downhill.

8. When the path meets a forest road, continue ahead along the road. At a T-junction of forest roads go right. Soon a path crosses the road (at a signpost for Fort Farm). Here follow the blue arrow, turning very sharply left to descend a path. Bear right on a track to Goitre Isaf and there turn left down a road.

9. Ignore a lane to the right (for Goitre Uchaf), soon reaching a clear crossing track. This is the old railway, a platform being visible on the right.

10. The shorter walk turns left here, following the old track bed. This is not marked as a public right of way on OS maps (though it is on other maps – the map in Lampeter's town guide for instance) but is an acceptable one by custom and practice. In high summer the banks are awash with rosebay willowherb, a lovely flower which is often considered a weed in Britain but is the National Flower of Greenland where its true worth is realised. The track bed deteriorates, but is quite clear. Beyond a gate there is an embanked section and an old footbridge over the track. Where the track swings right to a farm, maintain direction along a narrow, now-grassy track. Go under an arched bridge then bear left to a gate to cross a fence. The old track bed now reaches the outward route close to the rugby field. Follow the outward route back to the start.

11. A worthwhile extension of the walk visits the village of Silian, but involves road walking. Continue along the road past

the old railway to reach the A485.

12. Turn left. The main road is surprisingly quiet, but please take care. Just beyond Pont Silian, turn right and follow the road into Silian, visiting the church [5].

13. Return along the road, but soon fork right for Llanbedr. Follow this minor road across a junction then uphill into the unimaginatively named Lower and Upper Forests. The road then descends to reach the A482. Turn left, with care, to return to Llanbedr Pont Steffan.

Refreshments

There is an excellent choice in Llanbedr Pont Steffan.

Aberaeron

OS Maps:	Landranger Sheet 146 (Lampeter and Llandovery) Explorer Sheet 198 (Cardigan & New Quay/ Aberteifi a Cheinewydd)
Start:	The Tourist Information Office, Quay Parade, Aberaeron
Access:	Aberaeron sits at the mouth of Afon Aeron, at the junction of the A487 and A482 to the south of Aberystwyth. Buses link it to coastal towns north and south, and inland to Llanbedr Pont Steffan.
Parking:	There are car parks close to the beach near the Information Office, at the inner harbour, and near the harbour's southern pier
Grade:	Moderate. A long route but on good, or well-signed, paths

Points of Interest:

1. The Sea Aquarium has 22 tanks stocked with fish species found in Cardigan Bay and a further two large open tanks. There is also an open pool which is a reproduction of the rock pools that visitors might find on the beach. There is also a vast mural of life-size fish and a video exploring aspects of marine life as diverse as the Great White Shark and the work of local fishermen. The aquarium also offers coastal voyages in the *Sea Leopard*, a 33ft (10m) rigid inflatable boat. Visitors on the journey will see numerous species of sea bird and, if they are lucky, seals and dolphins. The aquarium also has a fascinating collection of photographs of old Aberaeron, shot on glass plates in the 19th century by local photographer Percy Lloyd.

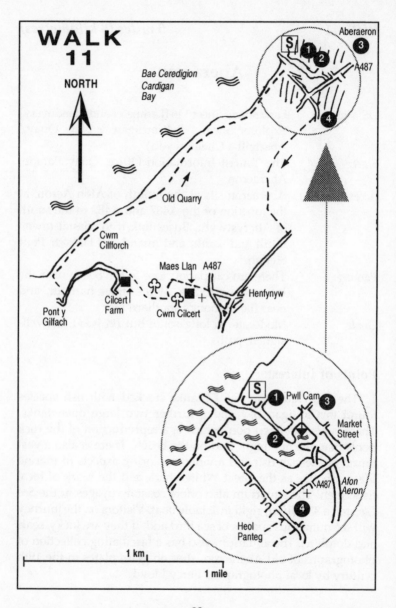

WALK 11

NORTH

Bae Ceredigion
Cardigan Bay

Aberaeron

S ① ② ③
A487

④

Old Quarry

Cwm Cilfforch

Maes Llan   A487

Cilcert
Farm

Cwm Cilcert

Henfynyw

Pont y
Gilfach

S ① Pwll Cam ③

Market
Street

②

Afon
Aeron

A487

④

Heol Panteg

1 km

1 mile

2. The Honeybee Exhibition explores the life of honey and bumble bees and has a collection of antique honeypots. The shop sells honey, honey-based cosmetics and beeswax polish and candles. There is also a cafe and licensed restaurant.

3. Aberaeron's modern story begins in 1807 when the Rev. Alban Thomas Jones Gwynne was given permission, by an Act of Parliament, to build two piers at the mouth of Afon Aeron. Though there was already a fishing village close to a bridge over Afon Aeron, the piers and the harbour they helped create rapidly transformed it into a prosperous shipbuilding centre and herring fishing port. The shipbuilding, which was centred on the south side of the harbour where the Yacht Club House now stands, was not confined to fishing or coastal vessels, with ocean-going schooners also being built at the town. The effect of this sudden prosperity was to produce a new, well-ordered town almost exclusively in Regency/Georgian style giving Aberaeron an almost unique elegance for a Welsh port. Any walk around the town's elegant streets is worthwhile. A walk in August on Bank Holiday weekend, during Aberaeron Carnival, is particularly good. The town claims that there are only two August carnivals worth considering in Britain – Notting Hill and Aberaeron.

4. The Aberaeron Craft Centre in Clos Pengarreg Courtyard has a number of workshops where artists and craftworkers can be observed, and completed works can be brought.

Walk Directions   [-] denotes Point of Interest

1. From the Information Centre walk along Quay Parade, passing the Sea Aquarium [1] to reach the Honeybee Exhibition [2]. Now walk around Pwll Cam, the inner harbour. To the left on its townside is Market Street and the County Hall whose ground floor was once an open-arcaded market hall. This is a good place to start an exploration of Aberaeron [3].

2. On the far side of the harbour cross the delightful footbridge over Afon Aeron and walk up to Bridge Street. Turn right, passing Holy Trinity Church on the left. Ignore the first left turn, but take the next, Heol Panteg.

3. Opposite an entrance to the Aberaeron Craft Centre [4] (to the left) turn right along a signed track beside a house called 'Craig y Mor'. Follow this enclosed track to its end where a stile gives access to a field. Follow the field edge, on the left, to reach a stile on to a road.

4. Turn right and follow the road into the village of Henfynyw, turning right at a road junction to reach the A487 opposite the Sanctuary Church of St David in front of which there is a bus lay-by.

5. Cross the main road with great care and take the signed track along the right side of the church, pausing to admire the magnificent lich/entrance gateway to the churchyard.

6. The track leads to a house (Maes Llan). Stay right to avoid invading the owners' privacy and to take a narrow path between a wall/bank on the right and a paddock fence on the left. Follow this path around the paddock to a stile. Cross and descend a shaded path to a footbridge in lovely little Cwm Cilcert.

7. Cross the bridge and ascend to a stile. Cross this and the field beyond to a (presently unseen) stile about 50 metres to the left of the visible gate. Cross and turn right along a green lane. Go over another stile and walk past Cilcert Farm, to the left, descending to reach a stile and a short footbridge. Turn left and follow the edge of the field beyond to reach a stile on to a road.

8. Turn right and follow the road as it descends. As you approach the houses near Pont y Gilfach, look for a gate on the right beside which there is a waymarked stile. Cross this, go over the rise ahead and descend steeply to a break in the

bracken where a stile gives access to the coastal path.

9. Follow the path to steps which descend to Cwm Cilfforch, taking the rough track up out of the valley and continuing along the cliff top. Ceredigion's coast may not have the epic grandeur of the Cornish granite coast or the picturesque qualities of Pembrokeshire's sculpted limestone cliffs, but it is still wonderful country and this rolling section of it is especially fine.

10. As you near an old quarry, bear left of the track on to a path which soon crosses a footbridge and then climbs steps to reach a stile. Follow the fence on the right, crossing two more stiles to reach another footbridge. The path now has a fence on the left, but soon descends towards Aberaeron, reaching an enclosed path beside the first houses (or the pebbled beach as an alternative) and the car park by the south pier.

11. Walk around the outer harbour, recrossing the footbridge to reach Pwll Cam and the outward route.

Refreshments

There is something for every taste and pocket in Aberaeron.

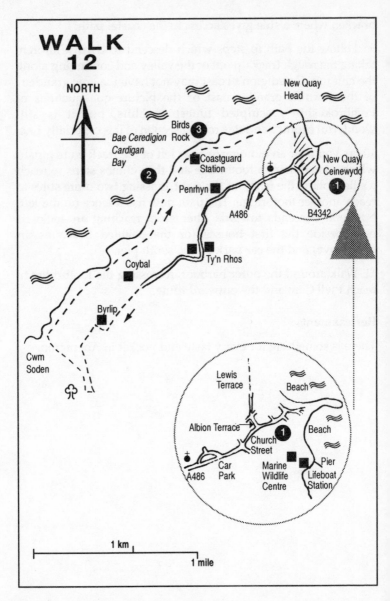

WALK 12

NORTH

Bae Ceredigion Cardigan Bay

New Quay Head

Birds Rock ③

Coastguard Station

Penrhyn

A486

New Quay/ Ceinewydd ①

B4342

②

Ty'n Rhos

Coybal

Byrlip

Cwm Soden

Lewis Terrace

Beach

Albion Terrace

Church Street

①

Beach

Marine Wildlife Centre

Car Park

A486

Pier

Lifeboat Station

1 km

1 mile

Ceinewydd (New Quay)

OS Maps:	Landranger Sheet 145 (Cardigan/Aberteifi and Mynydd Preseli)
	Explorer Sheet 198 (Cardigan & New Quay/ Aberteifi a Cheinewydd)
Start:	The Tourist Information Office, Wellington Place, New Quay
Access:	Ceinewydd lies at the end of the A486 which branches north from the A487 at Synod Inn. It is served by several buses.
Parking:	There is a car park close to the Information Centre and another beside the A486, close to the town centre.
Grade:	Moderate: Straightforward on good paths and roads, but long.

Points of Interest:

1. Despite the name, Ceinewydd (New Quay) has a relatively long history. It is first mentioned by an early 18th century Llanarth poet and again in an Admiralty survey of 1748. In the latter it is noted that a herring fishing fleet of 38 boats was operating out of New Quay and Aberaeron. The 'new quay' of the name is thought to have been Penpolion, a breakwater/ quay built at the southern end of the present beach, probably in the late 17th century.

Herring fishing was the little port's maintstay throughout the 18th century: it is recorded that on 5 October 1745 the local fleet caught 1,100 barrels of herring, almost $1^1/2$ million fish. Then, at the end of the 18th century a group of businessmen decided that New Quay was ideally situated for a ferry port for

Ireland and began to build a pier for ferries, intending to sail from New Quay to Wicklow and Dublin. The scheme came to nothing, the pier being unfinished, but the advantages of New Quay's sheltered, east-facing harbour were brought to the attention of other businessmen. In 1835 an Act of Parliament allowed completion of the harbour and there was soon a thriving shipbuilding business based around it. Soon the shipbuilding yards had expanded to employ hundreds of men as well as providing work for local blacksmiths, sailmakers, ropemakers and other craftsmen. New Quay's population rose to over 2,000 making it one of the most important towns in Ceredigion. The prosperity could not last, improvements in techniques and materials allowing larger ships to be built, these soon outgrowing the small yards at Ceinewydd. Fishing helped, but many craftsmen moved away. Fortunately the decline in local industry coincided with the upsurge in seaside holidays. Although Aberystwyth was the focus for the new visitors many found the more unfashionable New Quay, with its old world charm, an adorable place, a faithful clientele developing. It is the same today, New Quay attracting a loyal crowd of visitors, but a crowd which is increasing in size as its delights become better known. Having grown up over centuries rather than being planned and constructed as a whole, as at Aberaeron, and being on a steep rather than flat section of coast, New Quay has a maze of marvellous narrow, inclined alleys that just ask to be explored. One site definitely worth visiting is the Marine Wildlife Centre on Glanmor Terrace above the Lifeboat Station. Here the sealife of Cardigan Bay is displayed. The Lifeboat Station can also be visited. It was built in 1990, replacing the original station of 1904. Inside there are displays on the history of the New Quay lifeboat.

In September 1944 Dylan Thomas, his wife Caitlin and their children Llewelyn and new-born Aeronwy (a daughter named for Ceredigion's Afon Aeron) moved to a draughty wood and asbestos bungalow called *Majoda* (named from the owner's children Marjorie, John and David) close to the Aberaeron road from New Quay. Thomas hated the war and had spent its early years in Wales, at one time living at Talsun, also in Ceredigion, but had spent time in London after the Blitz because of his work on documentary films. By late 1944 he needed to be away from the conflict again. At New Quay he wrote much of his 'late period' work and almost certainly made observations of the local people which later surfaced in *Under Milk Wood*, his most famous work. The townsfolk mistrusted him – a Welshman who wrote poems in English, who wheeled flagons of beer home in the baby's pram and hid in the outside lavatory to avoid paying the landlord his rent – and Thomas wasn't too sure of them either. But he seems to have understood the local antipathy, writing to a friend: 'It is lovely here. I am not'.

In March 1945 the commando captain husband of the Thomas's next door neighbour came home on leave after a harrowing eighteen months behind German lines in Greece. He was immediately suspicious of his wife's friendship with the Thomases, probably because he though they were sponging off her, but possibly because he thought his wife was having an affair with Dylan. One night in a pub in Ceinewydd he quarrelled with Thomas and some of his London friends, and there was a scuffle. Later the captain, drunk and bitter, took a machine gun and grenade to Majoda. He intended to fire the gun over the roof 'to put the wind up those buggers', but in the dark and his drunken stupor he fired through the thin walls. He then went in and loosed off more rounds through the ceiling and threatened to explode the grenade. The captain was disarmed and later arrested and tried for attempted murder, but acquitted due to lack of evidence. Though Thomas was apparently the calmest of Majoda's inhabitants the incident terrified him, and the family soon left Ceinewydd.

Years later, after Thomas' death and after he had become famous, New Quay claimed to be the model for the village in *Under Milk Wood*. As early as 1939 Thomas had been inventing pseudo-Welsh villages in his stories (such as Aberbabel and Llareggub, the latter needing to be spelt backwards to get the joke – which his English publishers didn't). After his death the publishers of *Under Milk Wood*, who, belatedly, had got it, changed the name to Llaregyb, just about maintaining the joke but avoiding the profanity. It seems strange that New Quay and Laugharne (Talacharn) now vie for the honour of being the real Llareggub – such is the curiosity of fame.

2. Cardigan Bay is one of the best places in Britain to watch whales, and there are regular boat trips from New Quay. The bay has a resident population of bottlenose dolphins, and Risso's and common dolphins are also seen occasionally. Much rarer sightings include minke and humpback whales. Grey seals are frequently seen close to New Quay Head.

3. The cliffs from Craig-yr-Adar (Birds Rock) to New Quay, are some of the best places (some would say *the* best places) on Cardigan Bay for birdlife. Razorbills, guillemots and kittiwakes nest in thousands while, out at sea, gannets and manx shearwaters can occasionally be seen. Closer to the town the seabirds are likely to be black-headed gulls – look for the red bill and red legs, remembering that the birds only have chocolate brown heads during the nesting season. Rarer visitors include pomarine and long-tailed skuas, aerial pirates, but magnificent fliers.

Walk Directions   [-] denotes Point of Interest

1. From the Information Centre [1] head inland, climbing Church Street to its junction with the main road. Go ahead, soon passing a large car park on your left. Follow the main road past the town church (St Llwchaiarn's) to the right to reach the Penrhiwllan Inn.

2. Turn right and follow the minor road for about $1^1/4$ miles (2 kilometres) to where it ends at a farm track junction. To the right

the track leads to Coybal Farm, but we go ahead, beside the plantation, following a track which eventually turns sharp right to reach Byrlip Farm.

3. At the farm turn left along an enclosed track. This descends and reduces to a path through gorse and other rough shrubs. Follow the path as it descends more steeply to reach a path junction.

4. Turn sharp right along a path which soon reaches a footbridge, on the left, at a signed path junction. Do not cross the bridge: instead bear right, away from it, climbing gently along the wooded side of the valley of Afon Soden. Go through a wall gap and bear right to reach a kissing gate.

5. Now walk with a fence on your right and a magnificent view of Cardigan Bay [2] on your left. Follow the fence to another kissing gate.

6. The next section of the walk is along one of Ceredigion's finest section of coast, with marvellous views to the sea and, later, the endless whirling of seabirds. Descend to cross a footbridge and climb to a stile. Cross this and follow the field edge on the left to reach another stile. Cross and descend to reach a path junction.

7. The path to the left goes down to a small beach – a worthwhile detour – but our walk climbs the steps ahead, then bears left at a signpost and follows the field edge to reach the top of a flight of steps. Go down these, cross a footbridge and bear right to reach a stile.

8. Climb with a fence and the sea on your left, crossing further stiles to reach an open section of cliff. Continue to reach the coastguard station on your right.

9. The best section of the coast is now ahead, the cliffs from Craig-yr-Adar to New Quay Head being one of Cardigan Bay's major seabird nesting sites [3]. Follow the path, with the cliffs

close by on your left. The view is so good that the arrival of New Quay's streets is likely to take you by surprise.

10. The path leads into Lewis Terrace. Follow this to a road junction and continue along Albion Terrace ahead. Where this ends at a T-junction with Church Street, turn left to regain the start.

Refreshments

There is plenty to choice in New Quay.

Cenarth and
Castellnewydd Emlyn (Newcastle Emlyn)

OS Maps: Landranger Sheet 145 (Cardigan/Aberteifi and
                 Mynydd Preseli)
                 Explorer Sheet 198 (Cardigan & New Quay/
                 Aberteifi a Cheinewydd)

Start: Cenarth bridge

Access: Cenarth and Castellnewydd Emlyn both lie on
                 the A484 to the east of Aberteifi. They are both
                 served by Davies Bros buses 460, 461 and 462
                 from Aberteifi to Caerfyrddin (Carmarthen).

Parking: There is a car park beside Afon Teifi close to
                 Cenarth bridge. A fee is payable here during the
                 summer. There is another (free) car park close
                 to the castle ruins in Newcastle Emlyn.

Grade: Difficult. Though on good paths and tracks
                 (and short sections of road) the walk is long and
                 has several climbs. The outward half is the
                 better half (though the final section along Afon
                 Teifi is exquisite) and could be completed as a
                 3¹/₂ mile (6 kilometre) linear walk with a return
                 by bus. Please note that there are no buses on
                 Sundays.

Points of Interest:

1. In 1188 during the tour of Wales he undertook with
Archbishop Baldwin to drum up support for the Third Crusade,
Giraldus Cambrensis (Gerald of Wales) visited Cenarth Mawr.
There was already a bridge over Afon Teifi, a church dedicated
to St Llawddog and a mill (and a most attractive garden

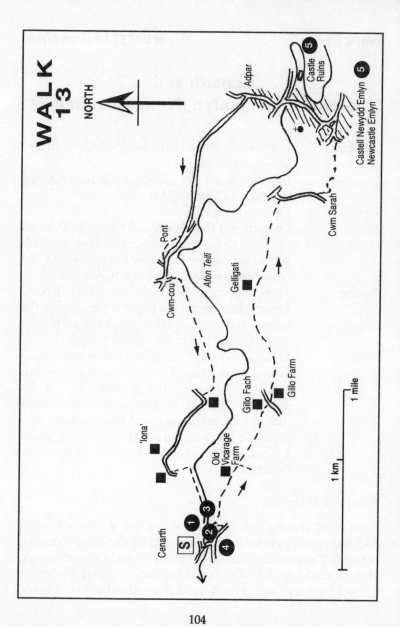

WALK 13

NORTH

Adpar

Castle Ruins ⑤

Castell Newydd Emlyn
Newcastle Emlyn ⑤

Cwm Sarah

Pont

Afon Teifi

Cwm-cou

Gelligati

'Iona'

Old Vicarage Farm

Gillo Fach

Gillo Farm

Cenarth

S

① ② ③ ④

1 mile

1 km

according to Gerald), but what really took his eye was the river. Gerald was a keen collector of miracles and curios, and Cenarth did not disappoint. He noted that in the river was a rock 'which St Llawddog hollowed out with his own hands' to create a 'flourishing fishing station'. What the locals fished was salmon and the abilities of the fish entranced Gerald. He noted that 'the waters of the Teifi run ceaselessly over this rock (that is the one hollowed by the saint), falling with a mighty roar into the abyss below. Now it is from these depths that the salmon ascend into the concave rock above, which is a remarkable leap, about as far as the height of the tallest spear'. Gerald concedes that 'this may seem hard to believe' but notes that 'it is the nature of the fish to perform such feats'.

For centuries after Gerald's visit Cenarth was a famous spot for salmon fishing: parts of medieval fish traps are still occasionally discovered. Interestingly seals which chased the salmon upriver, were occasionally seen as far inland as the Cenarth rocks. Today it is more famous as a beauty spot, the view of the rapids from the car park being superb, but salmon do occasionally still reach Cenarth.

Gerald also notes that at the time of his visit, Afon Teifi was the only river in England and Wales in which beavers could still be found.

It is not known when the bridge Gerald saw was built, or when it collapsed or was dismantled, but the present picturesque structure dates from the 18th century. It was built by William Edwards, a noted builder of Welsh bridges. It is said that the cylindrical holes were to reduce the weight of masonry, but they also have the advantage of reducing water pressure in times of flood. Interestingly, there is a legend that when Owain Glyndŵr's men were on their way to capture the castle at Castellnewydd Emlyn, they forded Afon Teifi at Cenarth implying that, at that time, there was no bridge.

2. Boats similar to the coracle are known from across the world, the idea of lashing an animal skin to a framework of branches

being a reasonably obvious one. Some experts believe that, consistent with this international history, the name derives from the Latin *carsula*, a little basket. In Wales the earliest *cwrwgl* (coracles) was made of willow and hazel twigs woven to form an open basket across which a skin would be stretched. Horse hide was apparently better than cow hide. Later, flannel was used, coated with pitch, tar and tallow. Today's coracles use calico proofed with pitch, though the woven framework remains much as it has for centuries. The fisherman carries a coracle on his back and then sits on an ash board secured across the top of the framework. To fish for salmon usually two coracles were used with a net slung between them, though some fisherman preferred to operate alone. Coracles draw very little water, making them ideal for a river with frequent shallows, but they are also very unstable, requiring enormous skill from the fisherman. Strong salmon could drag a coracle a long way before tiring, and all that time the boat could be upset.

The coracle is now used only on Afon Teifi and Afon Tywi, the Tywi boat being oval, while the local boat has a flattened bow. Coracles are driven by a single paddle swept back and forth across the bow. It is a relatively inefficient stroke – and paddling upstream is hard work – but gives the coracle amazing manouevrability in expert hands. Despite being hard work to move, coracles have completed remarkable journeys. Luke Hughes, a Wye coracle fisherman, paddled his coracle to Lundy Island and back in two weeks of glorious weather nearly 300 years ago. It was a marvellous achievement and he was feted on his return but history records that he was accompanied by a boat at all times, so rescue was at hand; and that he was picked up by a warship at Bristol, the crew of which was so impressed that a very long and very hard party ensued. One source suggests that this occurred on the way out, not on the return and that, as a consequence, Bristol rather than Lundy may have been the real terminal point of the journey. More definitely, in 1974 Bernard Thomas crossed the English Channel in 13^1/2 hours.

The National Coracle Centre explores the history of the boat, with examples of similar craft from all over the world, and its use on Afon Teifi. Beyond the centre is Cenarth's 17th century flour mill. There was a mill at the village when Gerald came in 1188, probably on this site. By the 17th century there were two, remains of the other still being detectable by the expert eye at the head of the Cenarth gorge. The present mill operated until 1939 but then fell into disrepair. It has now been renovated. The National Coracle Centre occupies what was once the mill workshops and the mill owner's pig sty.

3. The Three Horses Inn was built in the early 19th century as a coaching inn and Royal Mail horse change station, the mail coach from Caerfyrddin (Carmarthen) to Aberteifi (Cardigan) stopping here and at two other stations in its 30 mile (50 kilometre) journey. Beside the inn is the old village alehouse. Such alehouses provided refreshment to churchgoers from outlying farms, a much appreciated idea. The alehouses, often called church alehouses or simply church houses, made a profit from the ale they brewed and sold, this helping the upkeep of the church.

Opposite the Three Horseshoes is a complex of buildings with an interesting history. The old vicarage, with its pointed windows, was later the village school and schoolmaster's house. When a new schoolhouse was built the old building became a blacksmith's forge, shoeing the horses of the coaches which stopped at the inn. The buildings now house a craft and gift shop, and a small museum with the original smithy equipment and other period items.

4. As with the bridge, the church which Gerald saw has long gone, the present church of St Llawddog having been built in the 19th century. The earliest church on the site was that of the saint himself, built in the 6th century, and there was certainly a Norman church from which a font bowl, carved with human faces and dated to 'the 12th century, survives. The bowl was

returned to the church only a hundred years or so ago, having been discovered in use as a pig trough at a local farm. In the churchyard there is a curious three-faced stone with an inscription which, translated, reads 'Curcagnus, son of Andagellus', dating it to the immediate post-Roman period.

The stone, a conical, ice-sculpted boulder of millstone grit, is known as the Gellidywyll Stone and has had a curious history. The name is from a local mansion where, it is claimed, the stone stood in the 18th century to mark the grave of the owner's favourite horse. It is said to have been moved to Gellidywyll from its original position in a local field still called Parc y Maen Llwyd (the field of the grey stone). However, the first man to note the inscription claims to have read it when the stone stood at Maenclochog over 20 miles (32 kilometres) away.

5. The 'new castle' which gave Emlyn the addition to its name was probably built in the mid-13th century by Maredudd ap Rhys, son of Rhys ap Gruffudd, who successfully fought the Normans, defending Ceredigion against them for much of the early part of that century. Maredudd's castle was in stone, one of very few in south-west Wales to be constructed in that material, and almost certainly replaced the motte and bailey castle that lies to the south of Cenarth bridge. Maredudd's son, Rhys ap Maredudd, held the castle in 1287, but in the following two years it changed hands several times as the Normans strove to exert their authority on the area. With Rhys finally defeated and killed, the castle remained in England hands, the next century seeing significant refurbishment and extension. It was during this period that the town grew up beside the castle. In early July 1403 the castle was taken by followers of Owain Glyndŵr. It was a bloodless coup, the keeper, Jenkin ap Llywelyn, wisely surrendering the castle without a fight when faced with a rampant army of Glyndŵr followers whose progress through mid-Wales had been irresistible.

After Glyndŵr's time the castle fell into disrepair, being described as ruinous in 1428. It was refurbished by a new owner, Rhys ap Thomas, and saw action in the Civil War when it was held for Parliament until 1644 when it was captured by Royalists under Sir Charles Gerard. A Parliamentary force under Major-General Rowland Laugharne besieged the castle in 1645, but Gerard was made of stern stuff. Opening the castle gates, his men attacked the Roundheads and in a fierce battle routed them. Only when the Royalist cause was finally lost was Castellnewydd Emlyn surrendered. Then, as elsewhere, the castle was 'slighted', its walls destroyed by gunpowder and cannon fire so that it could never again be a stronghold against Parliament. After the destruction, the castle became a convenient quarry for locals expanding the town beneath its walls, so that today only gaunt remains of walls, and arches survive, a picturesque group of ruins overlooking Afon Teifi.

The town beneath the ruins is a pretty place. After the ruin of the castle it became a successful market town and still has an air of prosperity. It also has a couple of curious claims to fame. In 1814 it was the scene of the last duel in Wales when 'gentle' John Beynon shot Thomas Heslop dead, and in the same year is said to have seen the death of the last Welsh dragon. The venomous dragon apparently lived in the river beneath the castle and made a nuisance of itself in typical dragon ways until Rhys, a local veteran of the Napoleonic Wars, under cover of a red cloak, approached it by wading across the river. He shot the dragon and safely escaped, but the dying dragon shredded the cloak and then stained the river red and green with its blood and poison. It is a curious story for several reasons – how can a man hope to camouflage himself in a river by wearing a red cloak? And as 1814 is recent enough to be part of recorded history, what was the real event that underlies the tale of heroic Rhys the dragonslayer? But more curious still, the story seems to be an echo of the last days of Glyndŵr's rebellion. After the capture of Castellnewydd Emlyn Glyndŵr's forces moved south, taking Caerfyrddin (Carmarthen) on 6 July 1403 – which was also surrendered without a fight – and continuing to Talacharn

(Laugharne) where the castle was held by Thomas, Lord Carew. The Welsh arrived on 10 July and clearly expected to be handed the castle as had happened to the north, but Carew was a brave and accomplished soldier. Not only did he refuse to surrender, but he anticipated a Welsh flanking manoeuvre prior to a siege and ambushed them, killing a 700-strong force to the last man. Later in the rebellion Carew retook Castellnewydd Emlyn and threw Glyndŵr's red and green flag into Afon Teifi. It has been suggested that this flag and the shredded red cloak, signifying the death of the Welsh red dragon, are the basis of the dragon tale.

Walk Directions   [-] denotes Point of Interest

1. From the car park beside Afon Teifi [1] cross Cenarth Bridge and follow the A484 uphill passing a path, on the left, to the National Coracle Centre and the old mill [2].

2. Continue along the main road passing the Three Horseshoes Inn [3], on the left, to reach a path, also on the left, into the churchyard. Take this, passing in front of the church [4] and continuing to reach a gate and excellent stile. Cross and turn left along a lane. The lane reaches a house and bears right to reach another: just before this second house turn right along a narrow enclosed path, a signed bridleway.

3. Now follow a field edge (hedge to your right) with a view – to the right – of the motte of the early castle at Cenarth (see Walk 14). Go through a gate in the field corner and follow a track to Old Vicarage Farm.

4. Follow the track beyond the farm but, where it turns sharp right, go straight ahead through pens to reach a green lane. Follow this to reach a crossing lane. To the left is Gillo Fach, but we turn right, soon reaching the main road (A484).

5. Cross, with care, and walk along the farm drive opposite, following it to Gillo Farm. Just before the farm, turn left along

110

another green lane, keeping left when it passes an old quarry – to the right – and negotiating a fence by a gate on the left.

6. Beyond the farm building of Gelligati the lane becomes metalled: continue along it to reach a minor road. Turn right along the road for 400 metres then, as the road bends gently right, turn left and descend a track into the valley of Nant Sarah. Cross the stream by ford or footbridge and continue along the track, climbing steeply at first, then crossing a shallow ridge and descending to reach a road. Turn left, soon reaching the main road (A484).

7. Turn right, with care, but soon turn left along Porth Street, Castellnewydd Emlyn [5].

For those returning to Cenarth by bus, the walk ends here. Those returning on foot continue as follows:-

8. Continue along Sycamore Street and Bridge Street. On the far side of the bridge bear left into Adpar, where the first printing press in Wales was set up by Isaac Carter in 1718.

9. Bear right, uphill, on the B4571. Follow this road for 350 metres, then look for a house on the right with three distinctive dormer windows. Turn left opposite this. The road is called Parc y Trap, but is unmarked: look for a postbox set in the wall of a barn a few steps in on the left.

10. Follow this lovely road, shaded by arched trees. The road ends at a T-junction with the B4333. Just before this, turn right along a 'No Through Road' which cuts a corner of the main road. On reaching the main road again, turn right, uphill, into Cwm-cou.

11. Turn first left (Lôn Drewen, a 'No Through Road') and follow it downhill past houses and a fine chapel on the right to reach an old mill on the right.

12. At the road end, bear left on a signed footpath. Cross an

elaborate stile and bear right, uphill, at a path fork. This path becomes very overgrown in early spring, but is usually cleared by local ramblers. Follow it uphill, eventually reaching a kissing gate into a field. There is another kissing gate diagonally opposite, but if there is a crop it is considerate to follow the field edges to reach it.

13. Turn left along the road beyond the far kissing gate, following it around a sharp right bend at Penwenallt Farm, then downhill to a stream. Now follow the road uphill, looking for 'Iona', a house on the right. Just beyond the next house, turn left along a signed path, following it down to Afon Teifi.

14. Now follow the river back to the start.

Refreshments

The Three Horseshoes Inn, Cenarth
There are also several options in Castellnewydd Emlyn.

Cilgerran

OS Maps:	Landranger Sheet 145 (Cardigan/Aberteifi and Mynydd Preseli)
	Explorer Sheet 198 (Cardigan & New Quay/ Aberteifi a Cheinewydd)
Start:	The Coracle Centre, Cilgerran
Access:	Cilgerran lies on the southern bank of Afon Teifi a few miles south of Aberteifi. Follow the A478 south from Aberteifi and turn left at Pen-y-bryn. Alternatively, take the A484 east from Aberteifi, turning right to cross Afon Teifi at Llechryd and following signs for Cilgerran Castle. The Coracle Centre is signposted from the village.
Parking:	There is a car park at the Coracle Centre.
Grade:	Easy. Good paths and short sections of road.

As it lies south of Afon Teifi this walk is in Sir Benfro (Pembrokeshire) rather than Ceredigion. However, Cilgerran castle was built to contain the Welsh within Ceredigion and so has a firm place in the history of this area.

Points of Interest:

1. The Coracle Centre is a fascinating place with excellent displays on the coracle and its use in salmon fishing (see Walk 13). Salmon were once common in Afon Teifi, but sea trout were also caught at Cilgerran, the Teifi being tidal to this point. Today the old use of the coracle at Cilgerran is commemorated in a race on the river each August. Downstream of Cilgerran, beneath the ancient bridge at Llechryd, a weir was built to aid salmon catching. In August 1843 a group of 300 Rebecca rioters

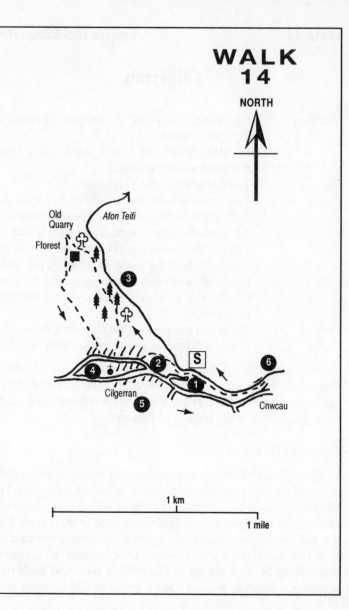

WALK 14

NORTH

Afon Teifi

Old Quarry

Fforest

3

2

S

6

4

1

Cilgerran

5

Cnwcau

1 km

1 mile

– protesters at the iniquities of the turnpike road system who took their name from the Biblical character – descended on the area and destroyed the weir. Their claim was that it was threatening the livelihood of the Cilgerran coracle fishermen, though in reality it was just another act of defiance. Abel Lewis Gower, a local man, who lived at Castell Malgwyn, now a hotel, who was the Governor of the Bank of England (and ancestor of David Gower, former England cricket captain) met the protesters and agreed that the weir would not be rebuilt.

2. At the time of the Norman conquest south-western Wales was the Kingdom of Deheubarth under Rhys ap Tudur, a situation which was confirmed in 1081 when Rhys met William the Conqueror during the latter's visit to St David's. William's journey was claimed to be a pilgrimage, but was much more likely to have been a show of strength. It worked too for, although the meeting agreed that Rhys would continue as ruler of Deheubarth, he was required to pay an annual fee of £40 for the privilege.

The agreement between the two men was shortlived. In 1087 William died, and soon after Rhys's position was threatened by other Welsh princes. Sensing his weakness the Normans reneged on the treaty and marched west into Wales, killing Rhys in a battle near Brecon. Soon the Normans had secured southern Pembrokeshire and were moving north, building castles at strategic points. The first were at Pembroke and Caerfyrddin (Carmarthen), but in 1108 Gerald of Windsor added another at Cenarth Bychan, a site now widely believed to have been Cilgerran. Gerald, an astute politician as well as a good soldier, married Nest, the daughter of Rhys ap Tudur to legitimise claims he might have on the land to the north of the Afon Teifi – the land of Ceredigion – but the marriage did not go entirely smoothly. Nest is renowned as the 'Helen of Wales', a woman of incomparable beauty who took a number of lovers, not least Henry I of England. In 1109 while Nest and Gerald were at Cenarth Bychan the castle was attacked by Owain ap Cadwgan, a cousin of Nest, who also had a claim on Ceredigion. With Nest's help Gerald escaped (by crawling down the chimney of the garderobe – in medieval castles the toilet facilities were merely a chimney, from the base of which a lowly servant was detailed to rake the accumulated filth periodically – a humiliating experience which did nothing to enhance his reputation), but she was captured. She seems to have been in no hurry to escape from Owain, striking a bargain that she would stay with him – almost certainly as his mistress – if her children were released. Gerald and Nest had four children, three sons and Angharad, a daughter who became the mother of Giraldus Cambrensis, Gerald of Wales.

South of Afon Teifi, the Normans were consolidating their hold on Wales by establishing groups of Flemish weavers whose allegiance was to the English crown rather than any Welsh prince. The existence of the Flemings was to cost the Welsh dear, their inability to control this part of Pembrokeshire leaving England with a constant back-door into mid-Wales. Initially, however, the tide ran with the Welsh, a combined Norman/ Fleming army being defeated at Crug Mawr near Aberteifi, in 1136. In 1155 Rhys ap Gruffudd become ruler of Deheubarth, but declined, at first, to submit to Henry II. Eventually he was forced to, but lost Ceredigion as part of the agreement. However, in 1170 Rhys regained Ceredigion and captured Cilgerran Castle (the first time that Cilgerran appears as the castle's name) holding it through two long sieges. Not until 1204 was Cilgerran retaken by the Normans, William Marshall, Earl of Pembroke capturing it in a brilliantly swift attack which caught the Welsh off guard. Llywelyn ap Iorwerth (Llywelyn Fawr) retook the castle in 1215, but it was a short-lived revival of Welsh fortunes, William Marshall retaking it in 1223. Then, in 1257 the castle was attacked by Llywelyn ap Gruffudd (Llywelyn the Last). Though the Welsh defeated an English army at Cilgerran, the castle remained in English hands.

Thereafter Cilgerran was quiet. It was refortified in 1377

when a French invasion of Pembrokeshire was feared, and may have spent time in Welsh hands during the Glyndŵr period. There is no record of action during the Civil War and by the 18th century it was a largely forgotten ruin. Its superb position and picturesque remains attracted the artists Richard Wilson and JMW Turner, but there was no consolidation of the stonework. That, and a slate quarry opened below the castle, caused it to become unstable, a long section of the curtain wall of the bailey collapsing towards the river in 1863. Only in 1938, when the castle was acquired by the National Trust, did stabilisation begin. The castle is now in the hands of CADW and is well worth visiting. In addition to sections of the outer walls there are the remains of two round towers and some domestic buildings, and the setting is magnificent.

3. During the last Ice Age the Irish sea was ice covered, the ice forcing its way inland to meet the glaciers flowing down from Pumlumon and the mid-Wales plateau. With drainage of the area impeded by the ice a lake formed in what is now the Teifi valley, though it was (in geological terms) a short-lived one. As the Ice Age ended the sea-ice margin not only retreated westwards, but northwards resulting in Afon Teifi having to alter its cause to the south in order to reach the sea. It was during the emptying of the lake and the subsequent change of course of the river that the deep, sharp-sided Cilgerran Gorge was cut. Today, with its tree-clad sides, the tight gorge is one of the most picturesque parts of the Teifi valley.

4. As with Cenarth, Cilgerran church is dedicated to St Llawddog, the 6th century Celtic hermit. The church has 13th century Norman origins, but only the tower remains from that period, the rest having been rebuilt in the 19th century. In the churchyard there is a stone inscribed in both Latin and Ogham (an ancient Brython/Irish alphabet of twenty characters formed by parallel strokes beside or across a continuous line). The inscription reads 'Trenegussus, son of Macutrenus'. The stone is

a grave marker dated to the 6th century.

5. The village of Cilgerran probably began around St Llawddog's first church and grew in prosperity below the imposing walls of the castle. In late medieval times it was an important wool market and also held cattle fairs in July and August. It is recorded that in 1800, 20,000 beasts were sold at one of the markets, most of them from pens in the main street. Later the Teifi slate industry added to the town's prosperity.

6. Though the quarrying of slate is usually associated with the great workings in North Wales – at Bethesda, Blaenau Ffestiniog and Dinorwig, near Llanberis – there were also quarries in other parts of Wales including here in the Teifi gorge near Cilgerran. It is not clear exactly when the first stone was worked, but there were active quarries throughout the 19th century: the last quarry was abandoned only in 1920. The extracted slate was taken by barge to Aberteifi, the same barges bringing lime for fertiliser and other materials upstream. At one stage an incline was built and a steam engine installed to drag stone up into the village where it was made into ornaments. There was even a slate turning house in the village. The Mason's Arms, passed on the walk, is still known as the Ramp Inn by some older residents because of its position at the top of the incline. An interesting sidelight on the quarrying is that, in 1850, complaints were made about the practice of dumping quarry rubbish into the river and its effect on fishing and the environment in general – an indication that environmental issues are not as new as some would have us believe. In response the quarry companies built a narrow-gauge railway to take the rubbish downstream. Of this nothing now remains, and even the quarries are being recaptured by nature.

Walk Directions   [-] denotes Point of Interest

1. From the Coracle Centre [1] follow the signed path for 'Castle and Village' up steps to reach the entrance to the castle [2].

2. Turn left, then right along a village road, heading towards the church. Before reaching it, take the signed footpath on the right, following it downhill and over Afon Plysgog. Bear right by the houses, then turn left to climb to a minor road.

3. Turn left, but soon go right, crossing a stile on to a signed footpath. Follow the footpath to a stile into a plantation of Douglas Fir and some broadleaved trees.

4. Follow the path through the woodland with occasional views of the superb Teifi Gorge [3]. The path eventually leads to Fforest Farm, formerly a manor house and once home of Dr Thomas Phaer, physician to Queen Mary and a noted literary figure in 16th century England. Phaer made the first English translation of the nine books of Virgil's *Aeneid*. He died in 1560.

5. Around Fforest Farm the walk follows a permissive path, that is a path which is not a public right of way but allowed by the landowner. Please respect this agreement: the future of the path is in your hands. Cross the lane and continue to a stile. Cross and follow the path beyond downhill to reach a track. Turn right, following the track downhill to an old quarry, on the right.

6. Now turn sharp left along a woodland path – you are now back on a right of way. Follow the path to reach the lane leading to Fforest Farm and turn right, following the lane to a minor road.

7. Turn left uphill then, soon, turn right to reach Cilgerran Church [4]. Follow the path past the church to meet the main road through the village. Turn left to walk through Cilgerran [5].

8. Follow the road to the Mason's Arm in Cnwcau (the hamlet at the eastern end of Cilgerran). Take the signed footpath beside the inn, following it downhill and turning sharply left to reach the river [6].

9. Now follow the delightful riverside path back to the start.

Refreshments

The Mason's Arm, Cnwcau.

Walk 15

a) Aberteifi   *1 mile (1.5 kilometres)*
b) Llandudoch (St Dogmaels)   *2¹/₂ miles*
(4 kilometres)

OS Maps:	Landranger Sheet 145 (Cardigan/Aberteifi and Mynydd Preseli) Explorer Sheet 198 (Cardigan & New Quay/Aberteifi a Cheinewydd)

Two short walks which explore one of the county's most important medieval sites and its most interesting town.

Walk 15a

Start:	Castell Aberteifi – Cardigan Castle
Access:	Aberteifi lies on the northern bank of Afon Teifi close to the river mouth, at the junction of the A487, A484 and A478 main roads.
Parking:	There are several car parks in the town, all conveniently placed.
Grade:	Easy. Town streets.

Points of Interest:

1. The first castle at this strategically important site at the mouth of Afon Teifi was built in the late 11th century by Gilbert FitzRichard, the Norman Earl of Clare. One significant advantage of the site was that the castle could be supplied by ship. This earliest castle, built in wood, was enlarged and strengthened over the next 100 years or so, but was rebuilt in stone by Rhys ap Gruffudd when he captured it in 1165. It was at the castle in 1176 that Rhys held the first recorded Eisteddfod. Remarkably, this involved not only competitors (in poetry and music) from all over Wales but also from mainland Europe. The

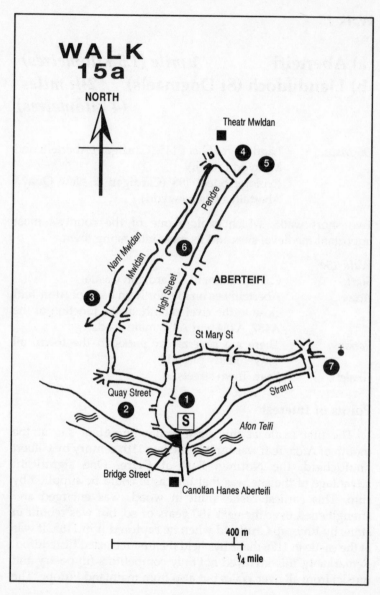

WALK
15a

NORTH

Theatr Mwldan ■

④ ⑤

Nant Mwldan

Mwldan

Pendre

③

⑥

ABERTEIFI

St Mary St

⑦ +

Quay Street

② ①

Strand

S

Afon Teifi

Bridge Street

Canolfan Hanes Aberteifi ■

400 m

¼ mile

prize winners were awarded a bardic chair.

The castle was refurbished and maintained throughout the medieval period, but was largely destroyed by Parliamentarian cannonfire in 1644. It is now privately owned. To the south of the castle is Pont Aberteifi over which the remnant Norman army fled the battlefield of Crug Mawr after their defeat by the Welsh in 1136. Legend has it that the sheer number of soldiers caused the bridge to collapse. Across the bridge and to the right, on Teifi Wharf, is Canolfan Hanes Aberteifi (the Cardigan Heritage Centre), which explores the history of the town.

2. Quay Street was once the busiest street in town with numerous merchants whose ships docked at the northern wharves on Afon Teifi. At the corner of Quay Street and Bridge Street is the Shire Hall, built in 1763 to replace the Courthouse and Council Chamber in the ruinous castle.

3. The old town walls followed the line of Nant Mwldan here, the brook being crossed by a long gone drawbridge.

4. The excellent Theatr Mwldan (and the town's Tourist Information Office) is housed in a (thankfully converted) mid-19th century slaughter-house.

5. To the left from here is the old County Gaol built in suitably formidable style in the late 18th century. It served until 1881 when it was converted into a police station and, in part, a private dwelling. A great local entertainment, during the building's time as a gaol, was that prisoners sentenced to incarceration after their cases had been heard at Shire Hall were marched in chains along the High Street to the gaol, while the townsfolk threw rotten eggs and fruit at them.

6. The Guildhall was built in 1858 and housed an indoor market. The clock tower was added in 1892. The field gun was captured during the Crimean War and commemorates the Charge of the Light Brigade which was led by Lord Cardigan. Though the gun is definitely Russian, it is not certain that it was

one of the 'cannons to the left of them . . . ' in Tennyson's famous poem on the ludicrous, but tragically heroic, action.

7. St Mary's Church is a fine building, originally constructed in the 12th century as the abbey church of a Benedictine monastery. The monastery stood on the site that is now occupied by the town hospital. The church was partially rebuilt in the 15th century. In the churchyard are many memorials to sailors lost at sea in the wrecks of Aberteifi-based ships.

Walk Direction   [-] denotes Point of Interest

1. From the castle [1] follow Bridge Street away from the river. The street passes through the site of the Teifi Gate in the old town walls.

2. Turn left along Quay Street [2], then right at the end to follow Lower Mwldan. Where Eben's Lane enters on the right, a short detour to the left is worthwhile [3].

3. Continue along Lower Mwldan, then Middle Mwldan and Upper Mwldan to reach, to the left, the Tourist Information Office and Theatr Mwldan [4].

4. Turn right to reach Pendre [5].

5. Turn right again, following Pendre to the Guildhall [6]. Ahead now is the High Street. The old town walls crossed here: our entry into High Street would then have passed through Bartholomew Gate.

6. Follow High Street past Black Lion Mews, on the left, then turn left along St Mary Street, following it to Church Street and the town church [7].

7. Return along Church Street, but turn left along Gloster Row and then right along Strand, following it back to the castle.

Walk 5b

Start:	High Street, Llandudoch (St Dogmaels).
Access:	St Dogmaels lies on the southern side of Afon Teifi, just a short distance west of Aberteifi.
Parking:	There is a car park just off High Street.
Grade:	Easy. Streets and good paths.

Points of Interest:

1. The present church was built in 1847, replacing an 18th century building which itself replaced the use of the old abbey church as the parish church. Inside there are two inscribed stones which were almost certainly gravestones from the early Celtic foundation of Llandudoch. One, at the western end of the church, is inscribed in Latin and Ogham (see Walk 14) and reads 'Sagranus, son of Cenotamus'. It is believed to date from the 5th or 6th century. The second stone, near the pulpit, is inscribed with a cross and spirals. There are other inscribed stones in the abbey.

2. In the late 11th century some of the monks in the monasteries of France had become disillusioned with the monastic life. The strict laws of St Benedict had become too relaxed, life was too easy, good living had replaced the harsh asceticism that many believed was the only true path to God. One monk in particular, Bernard of the abbey of St Cyprian near Poitiers, left his abbey to become a hermit. Eventually, gathering a few like-minded monks he set up his own monastery at Nogent near Chartres. Later his group moved to a new site at Tiron where they closely followed the rules of St Benedict, a harsh existence with a non-stop round of prayer and hard-work, with few comforts.

When the Normans came to Britain in 1066 they brought with them the traditions of French monasticism. At Llandudoch the Norman lord Robert FitzMartin found an ancient Celtic holy site and decided to found his own monastery, replacing Celtic mysticism with, as he saw it, a less deviant form of monasticism.

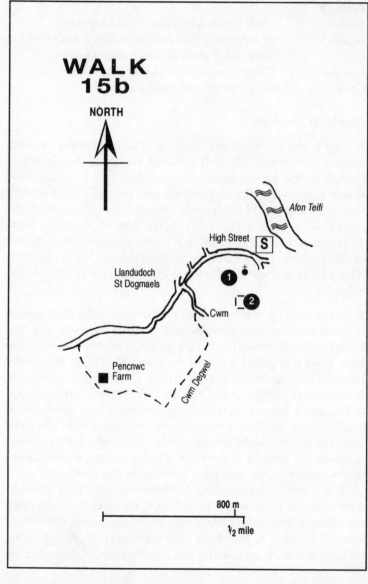

WALK
15b

NORTH

Afon Teifi

High Street S

Llandudoch
St Dogmaels

❶   +
           ❷

Cwm

Cwm Degwel

Pencnwc
Farm

|————————————| 800 m
|————————————| ½ mile

Dudoch was a 6th century Celtic monk, reputedly a great-grandson of Cunedda Wledig, founder of the royal house of Gwynedd, and a cousin of St David. Dudoch probably had a hermit cell (a *llan*) here in Cwm Degwel (giving the village its Welsh name Llandudoch) and around it a *clas* (a religious community, an early monastery) may have grown up. Recent archaeological work has revealed a curved rampart to the south of the present abbey which may have enclosed this early Celtic settlement. According to tradition, Llandudoch was attacked by Vikings in 988 and so it is possible that there were no monks here when the Normans arrived.

Robert FitzMartin endowed a new abbey, bringing thirteen monks from France to create one of very few Tironensian abbeys in Britain. The abbey was formally created in 1120 when Fulchard, also a Frenchman, was enthroned as the first abbot. The abbey remained a daughter-house of Tiron, but grew in power and had soon acquired its own daughter-houses, on Ynys Bŷr (Caldy Island), at Pill near Milford Haven and at Glascarreg in the south of Ireland. The early years of the abbey could not have been easy. After the Norman defeat at Crug Mawr in 1136 the tides of Norman and Welsh rule washed frequently over the area around the Teifi estuary and the alien French monks must have been occasionally concerned for their safety. Interestingly, though, when Giraldus Cambrensis (Gerald of Wales) came here in 1188 with Archbishop Baldwin, they were royally entertained by Lord Rhys and then slept at the abbey suggesting that there was by then little animosity between the monks and the Welsh.

At its height the abbey consisted of central cloisters surrounded by domestic buildings, the abbey church and a separated infirmary for old and sick monks. The abbey was dissolved in 1536, one of the hundreds suppressed by Henry VIII. At dissolution there were an abbot and just eight monks. As elsewhere, the abbey church became the parish church, the abbey buildings, strjpped of their roofs, deteriorated rapidly and became a convenient quarry for the villagers. What remains today are a series of evocative ruins, the ground plan of the abbey being clearly discernible and there being enough of the buildings to suggest the majesty of the place. The north transept of the abbey church, rebuilt in the 16th century, is particularly impressive.

Walk Directions   [-] denotes Point of Interest

1. From the car park, turn right along the High Street, then left to take the short detour to see the church [1] and abbey ruins [2].

2. Continue along High Street, passing toilets on the right, then turn left (Cwm) towards Cwm Degwel. Soon, turn right along a 'No Through Road' and, at its end, continue along the signed footpath, walking with a wall on your right and a superb view of steep-sided Cwm Degwel on your left.

3. Turn right through a kissing gate and follow the hedge on the right to another gate, continuing along the enclosed, waymarked path beyond to reach Pencnwc Farm.

4. Go through a waymarked gate at the farm and follow the farm lane to reach a road. Turn right and follow the road back to the High Street.

Refreshments

There is plenty of choice in Aberteifi and a selection in Llandudoch.